Mabel Wilcox, R.N.
Her Legacy of Caring

by
Barnes Riznik

Grove Farm Museum
Lihue, Kauai, Hawaii

Published by Grove Farm and
Waioli Mission House museums
Post Office Box 1631
Lihue, Kauai, Hawaii 96766

ISBN 0-9617174-4-0 (Paper back edition)
ISBN 0-9617174-5-9 (Cloth cover edition)

Dedicated to Kauai nurses - past and present

Contents

Foreword

Mabel I. Wilcox's life was extraordinary in its breadth, focus and purposefulness. Her legacy continues to this day in modern health practices and preservation activities on Kauai. Barnes Riznik, for twenty years the Director of Waioli Mission House and Grove Farm, has done extensive research into her life and career, as well as into the social and economic conditions of the times which influenced her. This is that story.

We are grateful to those individuals and trusts who contributed gifts and support. We acknowledge with thanks the help of Robert J. Schleck, Director and Moises Madayag, Curator of Waioli Mission House and Grove Farm museums in the research and organization of the photographs.

On this twenty-fifth anniversary of Grove Farm museum, the Trustees are pleased to present this book as a tribute to "Miss Mabel."

Ruth S. Smith
President, Board of Trustees
Waioli Corporation

Mabel Wilcox at Waioli Mission House in 1969 (Photo courtesy James Amos, National Geographic Society).

Prologue

Mabel Wilcox at age ninety continued her daily routines at Grove Farm in Lihue. The household and yard staff arrived at 6:30 a.m.; the sounds of wood being put in the iron stove in the kitchen and the hand-cranked coffee grinder producing fresh coffee acted as her alarm clock.

She would come downstairs from her bedroom, go out to the porte-cochere and check the thermometer and barometer, then look towards Mt. Waialeale to see what the weather conditions were like at the center of Kauai. She then would go out in the yard to meet the Grove Farm *luna*, Alberto Daguay, to discuss the needs of the gardens and her chickens, turkeys, and ducks.

Hisae Mashita, Grove Farm's cook, served breakfast in the room next to the kitchen. After finishing, Mabel would go onto the *mauka lanai* in the shade of the magnolia tree (her grandmother, Lucy Wilcox, had given the tree to Uncle George when he first moved to Grove Farm from Hanalei). Mabel would then smoke a Camel cigarette.

Her secretary, Masayo Ishii, would have arrived with the *Honolulu Advertiser* as well as the mail. Bills and organizational mail were sorted from the personal mail, and the personal letters were set out on the magazine table in the living room. Mabel took them to her couch to read, sometimes listening to the morning news on her portable radio.

Grove Farm's future museum curator and current director, Robert Schleck, remembers the first time he met Mabel Wilcox. "The screen door was opened by Miss Mabel, a small, quiet white-haired lady with gold-rimmed glasses, wearing a blue cotton belted shirtwaist dress, Chinese embroidered slippers, and a kindly hospitable smile." He reminisced later, "My memories of Miss Mabel are of a lady of great kindness and fun, interested and shy, but firm. There was no pretense or pomposity, and she seemed to prefer not to be singled out."

As part of her routine Mabel Wilcox checked and maintained the care of the buildings around her. As it had been for more than a century, much of the maintenance of Grove Farm was done by plantation carpenters, painters and plumbers.

Her routine was followed each day even after she broke her hip in 1975 and moved to one of the downstairs bedrooms. She died three years later at Grove Farm, leaving a legacy of caring; Ethel Damon, who knew her well for all of her nursing career, wrote years before, "No one knew Kauai people, their homes, their needs as she did."

Interior of the Grove Farm house, looking past Emma Wilcox's 1891 Chickering piano, through the 1915 parlor into the original 1850 house. The rooms had been opened up and served as a dining room and two small library rooms in the 1915 addition.

Introduction

During her fifty-year health career on Kauai, Mabel Wilcox, R.N., did more than anyone before her to shape institutional health reforms and improve the everyday health of people living on this small, rural Hawaiian island.

Mabel Wilcox's calling and her accomplishments in nursing in Hawaii were described by several colleagues and associates. Mabel Smyth, R.N., wrote about her career in *The Pacific Coast Journal of Nursing* in 1935, and Ethel Damon, the historian (and Mabel Wilcox's longtime friend), presented the story of her public health contributions in *Paradise of the Pacific* in 1952. These articles, as well as sketches by Margaret M. L. Catton and Frances R. Hegglund Lewis, introduce Mabel Wilcox as a significant health care provider, but until now there has been no full-length work that explores the historical meaning of her life.[1]

In 1911 Mabel Wilcox returned home to Kauai from the Johns Hopkins Hospital Training School for Nurses believing that the art of healing was founded on caring relations between health giver and patient. Steeped in Johns Hopkins Hospital's nursing ethos—a farsighted conjunction of curative medicine and public health—Mabel Wilcox's health care legacy was her professional commitment to both preventive medicine and clinical treatment. Only later would a separation between the type of medical practice concerned with the health of individuals and one concerned with social inequalities and the health of diverse populations come to characterize modern American medicine.

Though she may not have described herself as such, Mabel Wilcox held a feminist view of social and institutional health care reform during one of the most important periods in American public health history: she considered it a woman's mission to implement and carry out such reform in her community. Mabel's missionary family had been influential in the making of Hawaii's modern identity, furthering Western educational and Christian values, and creating a multicultural community.[2] She was representative of other middle and upper class women in her generation who mobilized voluntary groups, focused philanthropy on educational and public health issues, and participated in active cooperation with government authority.

Like other early graduate nurses in Hawaii, Mabel Wilcox faced broad challenges in merging local, regional, and national health care change. The nineteenth century's imported diseases had greatly reduced the Hawaiian population. From this tragic history, living conditions, public health, and infant mortality improved gradually through the 1900s. This book is about how medicine played a major and growing role in improving everyday life on Kauai. The early twentieth century saw a downward trend in tuberculosis death rates, a decline partly associated with such public health measures as modern sanitation and housing improvements, case screening, and the segregated care of hundreds of men, women, and children infected with tuberculosis. (Not to mention the epidemiological fact that tuberculosis may have become less virulent as the century wore on.) "It was slow, uphill work," Mabel Wilcox recalled of her days in field work and sanatorium management on Kauai, during what historian Mark Caldwell in *The Last Crusade* has called the "immensely encouraging and agonizingly frustrating" anti-tuberculosis campaign.[3]

During the 1920s, a second wave of health care reform brought a reduction in high maternal and infant mortality, a shift which occurred during a period of far-reaching demographic changes in Hawaii—changes which were the result of improved living conditions, healthier diets, and regular medical check-ups. The new "Well-Baby Clinics" Mabel Wilcox pioneered on Kauai for the Territorial Board of Health helped people accept and trust the advice and care of doctors and nurses. Although non-Western beliefs and ethnic identification continued to be strong among older and recent immigrants, many of whom were brought to Kauai to work on the sugar plantations, scientific and educational programs of maternal and infant care became more prevalent. These changes in health care symbolized the reduction of uncertainty and fear of illness in the everyday lives of people on the island.[4]

Mabel Wilcox planned and directed two hospital facilities on Kauai in her lifetime that expanded the horizon of prescriptive treatment. She planned the County government's new tuberculosis sanatorium, opened in Kapaa in 1917, and spearheaded the building of an independent, modern 94-bed acute care hospital in Lihue that opened to patients in 1938. Both were places of professional care and management, operated with high nutritional standards and fitted with up-to-date technology. In helping organize the Samuel Mahelona Memorial Hospital for tuberculosis care and the G.N. Wilcox Memorial Hospital, Mabel Wilcox acted on her sense that there was nothing more significant in shaping a hospital's internal life than the selection, continued education and support of its nurses. In particular, she witnessed how nurses helped patients overcome their prejudices and superstitions about hospitals as *make* houses—places where people were taken to die.[5]

During the First World War, from 1917 to 1918, "Miss Mabel," as she was known on Kauai, served in the American Red Cross in France. She experienced the plight of mothers and children as the nurse-in-charge at Salle Franklin, the Red Cross Children's Bureau Health Center in Le Havre for Belgian and French refugees. Salle Franklin was one of a number of such emergency clinics and hospitals for civilians built in France during the war and were regarded by American and French pediatricians as models for maternal and infant health care. Through her detailed diaries and reports, I have attempted to reconstruct how the impact of these wartime nursing experiences prepared Mabel Wilcox for the Territory of Hawaii's implementation in the 1920s of new national public health policies.[6] Her encounters in Le Havre with distinctions in class and the patronizing attitudes towards nurses also deepened her awareness of the realities graduate nurses faced. The First World War prepared Mabel well for the push and pull of the Islands' plantation company medicine, voluntary charitable associations, as well as resistance to women in the Territorial government.

This book offers an explanation of how health care changed on Kauai during the twentieth century and suggests why the remarkable reforms in public health, plantation medicine, and hospital standardization in Mabel Wilcox's lifetime happened when they did. Today, confronted by the worsening health of many developing nations, the history of progressive health care reforms in Hawaii during the first half of the twentieth century is more relevant then ever. The history of Mabel Wilcox's life as a nurse, especially among Hawaiians and immigrant groups, holds even greater significance when one considers the problems of health systems in developing countries under increasing strain from war, AIDS, disease, high infant mortality rates, and famine.

Mabel Wilcox's work across cultural, gender, and class lines brought her face to face with ordinary people's health problems. Throughout her long service as a nurse, sanatorium hospital trustee, and Territorial Board of Health member, she pursued intertwined goals of preventive medicine and curative treatment. To reach these ends, she adopted the tactics of the nation's Progressive political reformers, combining the efforts of voluntary women's associations with government support, in effect using the power of her social position to improve plantation hospital care on Kauai. It is well recognized that there has been a bifurcation in the goals of American medicine and public health. As epidemiologist Karen L. White has noted, however, changes to "heal the schism" are underway. Mabel Wilcox's life is a useful case history in old wisdom.[7]

In working on this book, I have attempted to put Mabel Wilcox's notable contributions into an historical perspective by examining recent ideas in social history, as well as the history of American nursing, maternal and child health, and hospitals. Interpretive research provided me with a context for the study of the primary sources, particularly Mabel Wilcox's papers, housed and organized in the library of Grove Farm—once Mabel Wilcox's family home and now a historical museum. Along with the transcripts of numerous interviews with health care practitioners (conducted at Grove Farm by Ruth Smith soon after Mabel Wilcox's death), these sources and surviving material reminders—such as Mahelona and Wilcox hospitals and the domestic imagery of Wilcox Hospital's nurses' residence—bring to life Mabel Wilcox's approach to the dynamic realities of reform in Hawaii.[8] There are many other life histories of American nurses, but *Mabel Wilcox, R.N.: Her Legacy of Caring* is the first account to tell her story.

Mabel Wilcox's papers—along with the Grove Farm plantation, family, and home life records opened to the public twenty-five years ago—have been used to explore many questions: Who created the modern health care system on Kauai? How did they accomplish it? What was the reciprocity between Kauai's plantations, voluntary organizations, public agencies and the semi-private sphere in effecting these reforms? How was Grove Farm, the family's plantation, involved in the island's social welfare and health care reforms? What were the motivating aspects of her life? How did Mabel Wilcox's large family shape her character and spirit? How was she affected by memory of the religious and educational reform energy of her nineteenth-century Protestant missionary grandparents, Abner and Lucy Wilcox and David and Sarah Lyman? What were the influences of her uncle, George N. Wilcox—her most powerful role model? How did her mother and father, Emma and Samuel Wilcox, shape her principles and those of her two sisters, Elsie and Etta, who also extended values of caring into the larger community?

Like their uncle G.N., Mabel and Elsie Wilcox remained unmarried throughout their lives; the untimely deaths of two of their three brothers brought the sisters even closer. Mabel and Elsie found emotional support from one another, preserving their family legacy by collecting books and by restoring several family homes: the Waioli Mission House in Hanalei (with their sister Etta); the Lyman Memorial Museum in Hilo (with their mother); and the plantation homestead at Grove Farm. Mabel Wilcox's preservation of Grove Farm for today's educational and community use is part of the legacy of caring she left for Hawaii.

As a participant observer in her planning of Grove Farm, I've used first-hand knowledge to explore the historical preservation of her life and the people who advised her in the 1960s and 1970s. Mabel's home, Grove Farm, and other places on Kauai provide tangible continuity of Mabel's legacy of caring. They are sites at the foundation of memory.

Memory is also made up of collective remembering and individual interpretation. Many have shared their observations and insights into Mabel's life for this biography, and I am grateful to them, but it has been my search for the historical meaning of her life that has given the book its shape.

PART I 1882–1911

Chapter One

WHERE TWO WORLDS MET

As her pregnancy came to term Emma Wilcox wrote to her mother, Sarah Lyman, in Hilo about home birth preparations for the arrival of her sixth child on Kauai. A nurse-governess would be coming from Honolulu to Kauai to help take care of the baby and the other Wilcox children. Only a day before giving birth, Emma notes, "Miss Ludgate wrote that she would come just as soon as we wished, so I write to her today, asking her to come right away."

Emma had cleaned the rooms of the plantation house thoroughly. "The parlor looks nice," she wrote. Emma had hung several new still life paintings and a landscape of Sam Wilcox's boyhood home—Waioli Mission House—on the walls. They were gifts of a visiting San Francisco artist, Margaret Girvin Gillin, who also had made small portraits of several of their children: Ralph, Etta, and Elsie.[1]

St. David Gynlais Walters, M.D., was Emma's Edinburgh-trained doctor in Lihue. He had assured her that she would not give birth for a few more weeks, but that afternoon she began to feel pains. "We went to bed early," Emma told her mother. "I woke up at ten with little pains, but as Sam was already asleep did not waken him until half past one, when I told him to send for the Dr. as I feared the child was coming." It was a false alarm, Sam said to Emma, but when Dr. Walters reached Grove Farm she immediately was confined. "At half past five the baby was born just before the children were up," Emma recalled. Dr. Walters and Sam assisted with the delivery, and the baby was born on November 4, 1882.[2] Emma and Sam named her Mabel Isabel.

"I had nothing ready so Sam and the Dr. had to find things", Emma said. Sam sent to Hanalei for Mary Fredenberg, part-Hawaiian mother of their friend, Sarah Deverill. Mrs. Fredenberg took charge of Emma and the newborn while waiting for the Honolulu nurse to arrive. As Emma wrote her mother, Sarah Lyman, in Hilo, "She came right up and stayed until yesterday, she is a very good nurse." Emma added wryly, "This is our little surprise baby as she came three weeks before the time."

It was Emma's sixth pregnancy. She was frail, and at 33 she had been pregnant or nursing her babies almost continuously since marriage eight years earlier. Because Sarah Lyman was unable to make the long interisland voyage, Emma was grateful to Walters for his medical attention.

> I think I am getting better from this confinement than any time before. Dr. Walters has been very careful of me. I am not strong and he says I must take great care of myself. He kept me in bed 14 days and this week I am to spend on the lounge and walk around the room a little. Next week I can go around the house a little.[3]

Emma added that she and Sam were rejoiced to see Miss Ludgate. "We are very much pleased with her and she has taken right hold to help me. It is such a comfort to know there is somebody to see the children." Three weeks after Mabel's birth, Emma wrote her mother,

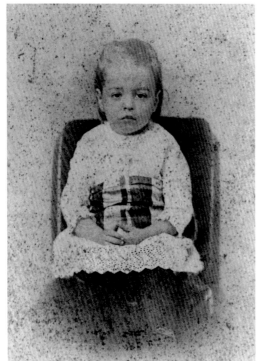

Mabel Isabel Wilcox at three years old.

"The baby has not been well for some days. Tuesday she lay with her eyes shut all day and crying … I feel pretty tired." Emma called for Dr. Walters who gave a spoonful of medicine and he "spent the night watching." Emma wrote.

A generation before Mabel's birth, the childbearing experiences of Sarah Joiner Lyman and Lucy Hart Wilcox—Emma's and Sam's mothers—were typical of other missionary wives in Hawaii. As new settlers they were intent on raising large families: Sarah and Lucy each gave birth to eight children. The frequent births—often a year apart—and the demands of their young children were exhausting: after one confinement, Lucy was not well enough to sit up for ten days, and Sarah had difficulty walking across her room four weeks after the birth of her first child. Both families lost at least one of their offspring: infant Clarence Sheldon Wilcox at one year of age, David Brainard Lyman at two, and Emma's older sister, Ellen, at 23.[4]

Expectant missionary wives had few choices for care during and after home deliveries, and husbands out of necessity often assisted them. Each island had an American missionary physician, and had it not been for these trained doctors, maternal and infant mortality might have been greater in missionary and other foreign families. There were no Western midwives in Hawaii with their accumulated experience to serve as birth attendants, and it took a full generation for many missionary parents to develop trust in Hawaiians like Mary Fredenberg to help them as their children entered the world.

Back in the United States, families like the Wilcoxes and Lymans could exercise the broadest possible choice caring for themselves, calling upon traditional midwives and Native American "doctresses" or hiring the services of male physicians. Many physicians were viewed critically, however, and historian Patricia Grimshaw finds this same skepticism among missionaries in Hawaii. She writes in *Paths of Duty: American Missionary Wives in Nineteenth-Century Hawaii*:

> Evidence would seldom support the idea that the presence of a doctor markedly helped in most cases of general illness, though the administration of morphine or opium was welcomed for severe pain. … Doctors tried a variety of cures, ranging from purgatives, bleeding, infusions of dandelion, courses of mercury, blisters, poultices, leeches."[5]

American missionary doctors were recent medical school graduates and most had been educated in midwifery during lecture courses in obstetrics. They had little practical experience, however, when they took up their mission posts. Yet most, if not all, of the missionaries' deliveries ended successfully. As the foreign population of Hawaii increased, missionary families became more and more reliant on their physicians since they were in close, everyday relationships with them, receiving medicines and reassurance. Intimate involvement in health care shaped family history and showed that in tangible ways their memories affected sensibilities and even responsibilities in the next generation.

James W. Smith, M.D., graduated from the New York College of Physicians, practiced for five years in New York City, then spent the following 40 years as the only Western doctor on Kauai. Smith responded to sudden calls to his Koloa home from mission stations as far away as Waimea to the west and Hanalei 50 miles to the north. On some occasions he was late to attend a birth. Abner Wilcox wrote Lucy in 1851, "I do not forget that this is dear little William Luther's birthday. One year ago today! No physician to help. Oh! What a day of trials and afflictions! Yet out of them the Lord delivered us." Four years later Smith wrote in his journal, "Started for Waioli. … I arrived at Mr. Wilcox's home about 6 o'clock—found Mrs. Wilcox with another son about 5 hours old."[6]

Albert Wilcox, Abner and Lucy's fourth son, was born in 1844 with a congenital deformity of his feet; one was turned outward and the other inward. Inexperienced in such matters and at a loss as how to treat young Albert, Smith, Gerrit Judd, and other physicians in Honolulu at first recommended shoes for his club feet, but five-year old Albert wore them with no success, much suffering, and continued lameness. Smith and Judd knew of an orthopedic surgeon with his own operating hospital in Boston, and the Wilcoxes were able to have the American Board of Commissioners of Foreign Missions pay for the cost of a 16-month journey for both Abner and Albert and the cost of etherized surgery on Albert's tendons. Albert survived the innovative, corrective operation without infection in Boston. Meanwhile back on Kauai, Lucy continued Abner's *Kula nui* or Select School for Hawaiian boys at Waioli. Both Abner and Lucy had been secular teachers in Connecticut.

Smith wrote her from Koloa,

We have selected 3 new *haumanas* [students] for your *Kula nui* [high school] … I think you will find Kaakau a good boy—Kalawa is also [a] pretty good boy—but rather too much disposed to be a Gentleman—I fear he will not like *ka hana maole* [real work]— I suppose both of these boys are well prepared to enter your school—the [other] boy which I had intended should go—& who is the most promising of the whole is sick ... I think he had better stay here near the *Kahuna lapaʻau* this year.[7]

In sad and appalling contrast to the experience of American missionary families was the everyday world of Hawaiians. Their lack of immunity to European and Asian imported diseases, lack of access to and trust in Western medicine, and their resulting devastating mortality rate provided a stark contrast to the general health of the missionary population. The Reverend Artemas Bishop in 1838 reported the formidable realities of Hawaiian infant mortality: "The great majority of children born in the islands die before they are two years old." O. A. Bushnell, the modern microbiologist and historian wrote in *The Gifts of Civilization: Germs and Genocide in Hawaii*: "Anyone who studies the history of Hawaii cannot doubt that, since 1778, infectious diseases introduced by foreigners have claimed more Hawaiian lives than all other causes of death combined."[8]

Hawaiian deaths outnumbered births throughout the nineteenth century. Even in the north shore valleys on Kauai—places that were isolated and sheltered compared with port towns on Oahu and Maui— annual reports from Waioli Mission Station to the American Board of Commissioners of Foreign Missions paint a grim picture of maternal and infant mortality. They show that in the Halelea district in 1837 there had been 84 deaths and 60 births. Progressive losses followed: in 1847 there had been 79 deaths and 39 births, and in 1849 there were 216 deaths and only 57 births. The population of the district was cut nearly in half; throughout the islands it is estimated that Hawaiian population declined by as much as 75 percent between Captain Cook's first contact and the year 1853. After several decades the American Board of Commissioners of Foreign Missions observed reduced enrollments in its mission station schools. Smith wrote of the problems, "We are ... painfully impressed with the fact that the no. of children is constantly decreasing. ... The school at Koloa," he wrote in 1858, "which 15 years ago numbered over 100 pupils, now numbers about 40."[9]

Infertility among Hawaiian women stood out in contrast to the high birth rate among missionary women. As Bushnell observed, "Children, formerly so plentiful, were no longer produced in numbers sufficient to increase the population, or even to maintain it at a stable level. A few Hawaiian women, to be sure, bore many children, a few had only one or two offspring, but most of them bore none at all."

There was constant anxiety about sickness and accidents at Waioli Mission Station. Abner Wilcox requested Smith to visit Waioli "as soon

as possible to prescribe for his eye which he had severely injured."
Lucy Wilcox wrote about illness in the schools and the problems of
others at the station, Edward and Lois Johnson and their children: "Mr.
W. had 12 boys out of school Monday with measles and as many every
day this week … I dread the whooping cough. I fear Mrs. Johnson will
lose one or both of her little babies." The Rev. Mr. Alexander had also
been discouraged by conditions among Hawaiians at Waioli.

> Dropsies are among the most frequent [diseases]; palsies and
> diseases of the lungs also occur; syphilis is rare, but gonorrhea
> prevails extensively. … Immoderate eating and fasting, living in
> damp huts, long exposure in the water, and sleeping on the ground
> are all assigned as causes for the many sick and weak among the
> natives.[10]

In 1850 Abner wrote Lucy from Honolulu about his fear of
epidemics:

> No cholera here as yet. I want to urge upon you the importance
> of having medicine at hand, Dr. Jayne's Carminative Balsam is
> thought to be a cure. … Everything depends upon being prompt.
> You will find directions in the almanac. … But I hope a merciful
> Providence will keep so great a scourge from the islands.[11]

On Kauai Western medicine did gain one notable, bicultural
success in the control of smallpox by missionaries; their vaccination
against smallpox disease was the most preventive function they
performed. During the *Ka Wa Hepela*, the smallpox epidemic on Oahu
that resulted in the death in 1853 of more than 5,000 Hawaiians,
previous missionary efforts of vaccination on Kauai and Niihau,
quarantine by the newly organized government Board of Health, and
geographic isolation of the two islands kept mortality to a minimum.
Wrote Johnson in his mission station report, "I judge that at least 3/4
of adults in Waioli field were secure, at least in part, from the ravages
of the disease by previous vaccination." The labor of vaccination
and re-vaccination was not inconsiderable. "In this work," Johnson
added, "I was aided by brother Wilcox; and received some assistance
from Hawaiians." Smith's journal from 1853 to 1864 records his
trips to vaccinate Hawaiian children around the island, and he wrote
newspaper articles in Hawaiian for *Ku'oko'a*, "The Independent,"
about health conditions of Hawaiians."[12]

On Oahu during 1853's severe smallpox epidemic, many ordinary
citizens volunteered to nurse the sick, and Hawaiian *kahuna lapa'au*
increased their efforts to give care and train healing assistants in

traditional medicine. However, as Bushnell concluded, the response of the *kahuna* in the nineteenth century to imported diseases was destined to be futile despite their training:

> No medical profession anywhere in the world ... was prepared either in philosophy or in therapeutics to combat microorganisms as the causative agents of disease. Nonetheless, the *kahuna lapaʻau* ... continued principles and practices of native medicine far longer into the nineteenth century than might have been possible without that program of intensive preparation.[13]

Cultural differences and prejudice separated Western medical practitioners from Hawaiians. "I must tell you something of my medical practice among these natives," Smith wrote from Koloa to his family in the United States in 1851:

> It is not so pleasant business prescribing for them as for more civilized people. They, as a general thing, have not patience to follow out a course of treatment. If a few doses of medicine cure a man—it is all well—if not he is off soon to some native doctor who has about as much correct knowledge of treatment of diseases as he has of Land in the Moon.[14]

"Year by year disease and death exerted relentless pressure on the islands' population. Failing in numbers and in vigor, the Hawaiian nation seemed to be plunging toward extinction," as historian Richard Greer has written of depopulation. However health workers in the United States and Europe had begun to organize the identification, treatment, and eradication of all of the most feared diseases of the previous century. In Hawaii this included American missionaries and other Western physicians creating hospitals especially for the support, care, and treatment of Hawaiians, including *Hale Maʻi O Ka Wahine Aliʻi*—the Queen's Hospital—by King Kamehameha IV and Queen Emma.[15]

American Protestant missionaries played a controversial role in the transformation of Hawaii during the nineteenth century, and modern-day generalizations about them betray a complicated legacy. Missionary defenders emphasize their achievements in Christianization and the promotion of literacy at the invitation of local Hawaiian rulers. Critics of missionaries interpret them as willful, assertive colonizers responsible for the destruction of the indigenous culture. There are others who describe a more dynamic relationship, emphasizing the manner in which Hawaiians absorbed Westernization while perpetuating their own traditions.[16]

Mabel's grandparents, Abner and Lucy taught their children about what they believed to be a crisis of history in the nineteenth century: It was, in their view, a conflict between worldly and materialistic interests, and the usefulness of Christian service as a response to that conflict. They believed *mikanele*, missionaries, like themselves had something more to offer Hawaiians than secular Western materialism in an expanding commercial world. Abner and Lucy, who were descended from pre-Revolutionary Protestant New England families, were convinced that they could teach regeneration by example. As teachers, they doggedly strove to shape Hawaiian lives in Christian religion and the teachings of the Bible. In a world of conflict between Native and foreign values, they felt that Hawaiians had a moral right to Western education. Abner taught missionary schools in Hawaiian, and he trained many Hawaiian common school teachers at his "Select School" in Hanalei.

Both Mabel's paternal and maternal missionary grandparents fully experienced the medical history of nineteenth-century Hawaii—its frustrations and fears, and its tragic effects of disease on Hawaiians—and this familial experience would define the two worlds into which Mabel later was born.

Reflecting on her missionary heritage, Mabel Wilcox would put it: "I got it from *both* sides."

Chapter Two

GROVE FARM

Thirteen years before Mabel Wilcox was born, a Wilcox family tragedy would occur that had lasting effects on the tightly knit group. In 1869 Abner and Lucy were able to make a visit to their families in Harwinton, Colebrook, and Torrington, Connecticut, Lucy's first to the United States in over 30 years. They took eleven-year old Henry as far as California where they stopped to visit Charles, their eldest son, who was working with Lucy's brother. In a prophetic tone about their kinship ties, Abner wrote to his other sons on Kauai, "Should we not live to return, it is your Mother's judgment and wish, that Henry go back to the Islands. … We have great confidence that among you all there is that brotherly feeling and attachment that raises you above all selfishness. … " Less than a month later, Abner and Lucy fell critically ill with a fever and died after the wearisome trip back to New England.[1]

Their deaths caused an abrupt transition in the family's life. As the eldest son in Hawaii—not yet 30 years old—George Norton Wilcox took responsibility as head of the Wilcox household. In 1964 he had leased and soon was the owner of one of the earliest sugar plantations on Kauai, Lihue's Grove Farm. In so doing, he also took charge of the family's financial and legal affairs and assumed care of his younger brothers. George Wilcox's parents' death was a critical turning point that drew the family together: He found a position for his brother Albert at Lihue Plantation and brought Sam to Grove Farm to live with him and manage the ranch herd. George Wilcox never married; instead, he became a devoted uncle to Sam and Emma's six children—Ralph, Etta, Elsie, Charles, Gaylord, and Mabel—as they grew up on Kauai.

Uncle George, or G. N. as he was best known, was a person of exceptional intelligence. In 1860 after graduation from Punahou

School, the missionary-built academy in Honolulu, Lucy and Abner had sent him to the newly opened Sheffield Scientific School at Yale, where he studied invention, applied research science and technology. G. N. came home to Kauai with advanced civil engineering knowledge and, perhaps more importantly, the confidence to meet agricultural and industrial challenges of large-scale planting, irrigation, cultivation, harvesting and processing, as well as techniques in bridge building and road making, and the uses of steam power. G. N. was one of the first young men raised in Hawaii to be formally trained in the technology that built the sugar industry, not to mention the modern infrastructure of Kauai.[2]

Like other early sugar planters and ranchers in Hawaii, G. N. lived where he worked. Yet home was truly where G. N. applied his greatest intelligence and love, and his nieces and nephews were the recipients of the care G. N. Wilcox took in creating his home. A drawing of Grove Farm made at about the time of Mabel's birth shows the simple homestead. Mabel Wilcox recalled Grove Farm's surrounding fields of sugar cane, the canehaul railroad to the nearby Lihue sugar mill, and growing up in the long, low house with its steep-pitched roof. Making a tent with her hands to describe boards and fence posts, she remembered piles of lumber stacked on end near the carpentry shop and the everyday uses of homestead outbuildings. "The yard was full of lumber and cattle and horses," she said. She told about oxen driven into the Grove Farm yard in the mornings and yoked to heavy carts, and horses that were pastured in front of the house: [3] "We all rode, we'd ride all over, and if we didn't get back by 5 p.m., my father was on his ear"—very concerned about the safety and well being of his children. There were wetland taro patches, rice farms, and a stream in the valley below the house running towards Nawiliwili Bay two miles away. Mabel remembered the simple cottages near the main house: the plantation office, her uncle's sleeping quarters, and a guest cottage. Another of the small structures was where Mabel and

Drawing of Grove Farm by Margaret Girvin Gillin. c.1882

her brothers and sisters were tutored. She turned it into her nurse's office in 1912, and later this was the temporary makeshift headquarters for the G. N. Wilcox Memorial Hospital administration during construction of the new hospital in 1937–1938.

As youngsters the Wilcox children learned to make their own amusements. Their regular playmates were the sons and daughters of William Hyde Rice and Mary Waterhouse Rice, near neighbors across Nawiliwili valley. Mabel said that she was a born tomboy. Though physically slight like her older sisters and brothers, she was a tree-climber who always went to the highest limbs with the greatest amount of daring. "My oldest sister was Etta, a very good student," Mabel said. "Elsie was awful smart. I was the dumb one, or thought I was." [4] All of the children were bashful. Florence Purvis, their governess from Scotland, commented on the acute shyness of the Wilcox children: "We all went to Mrs. L'Orange's today to her little girl's party and I am so tired. ... Island children are the hardest to get along with; there were Wilcoxes, Doles, Scholtzes and others there today and no one would speak or play with the others. The Wilcoxes ... all crowded around their mother, began to cry if anyone looked at them."[5]

Emma was busy as mother and wife, rearing the children and supervising the household help at Grove Farm. Her knowledge of infant care came from her mother in Hilo, from such popular advice

Wilcox children l to r: Gaylord Parke, Elsie Hart, Ralph Lyman, Mabel Isabel, Lucy Etta, and Charles Henry at Grove Farm. c. 1887.

books as *The Physiology of Marriage*, and from Beta Glade Isenberg, the wife of Lihue Plantation's owner, Paul Isenberg. Mabel recalled "Mrs. Paul advised mother on everything. Helped her a great deal at the beginning."

Dr. Smith, though now advanced in age, continued to care for the Wilcoxes when they were sick; George had the first two telephones installed on Kauai at Grove Farm so Emma could call Smith in Koloa about the children and her own frequent illnesses. Though Smith was retired by the time Mabel was born, he was called to care for Elsie a few years earlier. His journal gives a good description of some of the pediatric problems of the day:

> Sent for to see S. Wilcox's child—taken suddenly with diarrhea with bloody discharges—I could not go immediately and sent Dovers Powder in 1 gr doses believing the child 4 months old. Two hours later I found the child narcotized—it was only 4 weeks old—could be waked with difficulty & would raise a little & then fall to sleep again—this continued 10 hours. I then gave it coffee—made of the strength ordinarily used for the table & mixed half milk with a little sugar & soon all the drowsiness left—and the looseness which had been checked returned—NB one grain Dovers Powder is too large a dose for a child 4 weeks old.[6]

Mabel's mother accepted the limited boundaries of a woman's participation in a nineteenth-century *haole* marriage in Hawaii. Her marital duties—supervising rounds of housework, laundry, food preparation, and sewing for her husband, brother-in-law, and children—took priority over a long-held desire to teach music. Like her own mother, Emma did devote herself to being her children's spiritual guardian, transmitting moral norms through strict parental control.

Emma was disapproving of all forms of ostentation and social pretentiousness. The family lived moderately. They had simple tastes and only a few changes were made at Grove Farm in 40 years of Emma's residence there. In the U-shaped homestead compound, George eventually constructed separate sleeping quarters for himself. He also added a small, four-room cottage at one end of the house for Sam and Emma's growing family. According to Elsie, "Everything was simple. There were not many luxuries. People worked hard. The missionary tradition held. ... "[7] Mabel's parents and uncle were unassuming, and Mabel considered them "liberal" rather than evangelical in their Christian religion. Her mother had converted to Episcopalianism when she was at school on the mainland.

The family spent many evenings together, Uncle G. N. reading articles on agriculture, science and history, fiction, and poetry. A table in the parlor was stacked with piles of magazines including *Scientific American, Atlantic Monthly, Harper's, and St. Nicholas.* Emma frequently read aloud to the children. Mabel remembered Harriet Beecher Stowe's *Uncle Tom's Cabin* as a favorite; its warm sympathy and sense of inequity had laid bare the injustice of slavery before its abolition. Besides reading, music and art were Emma's joys, too. She sang and played the piano that she had brought to Kauai when she was married, and she organized "juvenile musicals" for the children and their friends.[8]

Emma kept two of her own original drawings from her school days at Punahou—one a floral drawing and the other a view of the academy. As art historian David Forbes observes of her pencil sketch of Punahou, it is "a wonderful primitive kind ... she was out there drawing every window and every shingle she could get on paper." Emma and Sam

Grove Farm plantation office with new addition. c.1900.

also treasured an early drawing that the noted Island artist D. Howard Hitchcock made of a mouse nibbling cake crumbs, with the title "The Last Guest at the Wedding." Hitchcock presented the drawing to the Wilcoxes in Hilo as a wedding present in 1874. Hitchcock was 13 years old at the time and a former student of Emma's.

She also brought a "cabinet of curiosities" to Grove Farm, filled with such natural wonders as shells, coral lava specimens, and a bat. Four Hawaiian quilts were included in her trousseau.

By the time of Mabel's birth, Uncle George was financially successful as a planter. He directed others decisively and managed with farsighted, energetic vision. Already the owner of Grove Farm, G. N. leased, then purchased, additional land from Princess Ruth Keelikolani to grow more sugar and expand his ranching operations. The acreage of Grove Farm increased tenfold from the 1870s to the 1890s. G. N. was known for his generous character, his caring of others and generous support of churches and schools. Henry Townsend, a teacher on Kauai from 1883 to 1885, recalled riding out to visit one of Grove Farm's workers' camps early one day with G. N., who said, "We get off our horses here. They have a little boy with a club foot [sic] at this house; and the doctor thinks he can straighten it. He is to operate on it this morning; and as the father was so awkward he could not make the necessary splints, I had to make them myself."[9]

Because G. N. and his brothers understood the health crises of Hawaiians, they later supported the first tuberculosis sanatorium in the Islands, Leahi Home in Honolulu, and continued to make periodic donations to it. Albert, too, and his wife Emma Kauikeolani Napoleon Mahelona helped to establish Kauikeolani Children's Hospital in Honolulu, which was named for her. Lihue's first plantation hospital was built by G. N. and the owners of Lihue and Kipu plantations in 1899. In these and other ways, the Wilcoxes demonstrated their deep involvement in public health in Hawaii. Such was the family mission to which Mabel Wilcox found herself drawn.[10]

Like other *haole* sugar planters, G. N. and Sam also participated in the Hawaiian government. When court sessions were held, Mabel remembered judges and lawyers from Honolulu arriving by steamer in Nawiliwili at two or three in the morning, to be taken up to Grove Farm for coffee and breakfast. Some stayed at Grove Farm and others with the Rice family. "The court would often stay a whole week," Mabel said. "They slept in the guest cottage with four beds. G. N. had a room in his cottage that was a guest room, with two beds." Mabel's father had been elected sheriff of Kauai before she was born, holding that office for 25 years. Sam Wilcox was in charge of visits by Kingdom officials. In addition, he was the Board of Health's agent for Kauai and Niihau, responsible for locating infectious cases of leprosy and tuberculosis on the islands. He was bi-lingual and well known.[11]

During King Kalakaua's reign, G. N. was elected representative from Kauai in the Hawaiian legislature. He served again from 1887 until annexation by the United States in 1898, during one of the most troubled periods of modern Hawaiian history. As Queen Liliuokalani struggled with the legislature in 1892, she replaced several cabinets and turned to Wilcox to become her Prime Minister. He chose a new cabinet, but after several months, the Queen proposed a vote of no confidence. Because of his opposition to a proposed national lottery and—perhaps more importantly—his opposition to a new constitution that would give the queen more ruling authority, G. N. was voted out.[12] In the following months after G. N.'s expulsion in 1892, political opposition to the Queen increased. Though G. N.'s brother Albert actively sought the Queen's overthrow and the annexation of Hawaii by the United States, his brothers, including Luther, who had become a government magistrate in Honolulu and a Hawaiian language courts translator, continued to favor the constitutional monarchy. G. N. later supported annexation, but he and other Kauai leaders such as Paul Isenberg and William Hyde Rice were unwilling to join those who deposed the Queen in 1893.[13]

Although Mabel was only eleven when the monarchy ended, her father and uncle introduced her in the coming years to the politics of Hawaii and the work of the Board of Health.

Chapter Three

MOTHER AND DAUGHTER

In 1876, after Emma gave birth to her first child, Ralph, at Grove Farm, Sarah Lyman wrote to her daughter: "You may now be said to have commenced your life work for it is a grand work to train up children for the Master." Such was the seriousness and depth with which Emma Wilcox was to greet motherhood—an example set by Sarah Lyman.

Emma maintained a caring relationship with her mother in Hilo. Typical of their affectionate feelings was a note Sarah had sent after Emma's wedding:

> I had it in my heart to write you and Sam a whole sheet of congratulations. ... I cannot tell you how anxiously we all waited for the steamer and how nervous I got before the mail came. I even capsized the teapot of hot water on the lunch table. ... [1]

Growing up in Hilo, Emma was sent to Punahou School for several years during her adolescence. She then taught at her father's Hilo mission school and attended Rockford and Dearborn Seminary in Michigan. After Emma's only sister, Ellen, died in Chicago, she returned home and married Samuel Wilcox. When Emma departed for Kauai as a bride, her mother was saddened by the prospect of no longer having her younger daughter at home with her. She cheered up when Emma later brought her firstborn infant Ralph to visit her in Hilo. Sarah. Lyman was nearly 70 when she wrote to her sister in Vermont:

> "I had a delightful visit of six weeks ... last summer, and shall I tell you that tending the darling boy *set the old clock going again ...* I hear often from Emma. Voyaging is hard on her and me, so we shall not meet often, I fear."[2]

It was not only voyaging that was hard on Emma Wilcox; throughout her life she was weakened by poor health. Mabel's relationship with her mother would grow more intimate as a result of Emma's recurrent illnesses and heart problems, and it was her mother's frailty that first quickened Mabel's desire to take care of others. "You see, I took care of my mother when she wasn't well. So often I wouldn't know what to do for her." Mabel always remembered this, and recalled saying to herself, "If I were a nurse, maybe I could help. I kept wanting and wanting to be a nurse."[3]

Mabel's commitment to nursing grew stronger because of her mother's needs. Even Mabel's educational career and expanding life experiences were as a result of Emma's illnesses. Though she matriculated at Punahou, at age twelve, Mabel and brother Gaylord accompanied Emma to Oakland where her mother found treatment. The siblings attended Oakland High School and spent time with their California cousins.

Meanwhile, Mabel's sisters, Etta and Elsie, were away from home enrolled at Wellesley College in Massachusetts. As Judith Hughes writes in her book, *Women and Children First: The Life and Times of Elsie Wilcox on Kauai*, "The Wilcox young women were part of a small minority of women in the United States receiving a college education. In 1900, only 2.8 percent of women between eighteen and twenty-one were enrolled in institutions of higher learning." At the turn of the century, Wellesley was regarded as one of the leading colleges for

Mabel Wilcox's room in Oakland while attending Oakland High School in 1898, showing an American flag in the center and a Hawaiian flag draped to the right.

women in the country, and Etta and Elsie took advantage of both its unparalleled opportunities for women, as well as the concerts, theater productions, and museums in nearby Boston. As Hughes observes, "At Wellesley, [Elsie] Wilcox experienced an all-female community, with friendship, support systems, and a sense of purpose. She later tried, with some success, to recreate something similar of Kauai."[4]

Mabel would reap the benefits of Etta and Elsie's experience. In 1900, Mabel joined her sisters on the East Coast, entering Dana Hall School (near Wellesley College) as a senior and staying till 1901. At the same time, Gaylord set off for Baton Rouge to study sugar technology and agriculture at Louisiana State University.

There were 30 other students in Mabel's class at Dana Hall, half of them from beyond New England. The school's principal was Helen Temple Cooke, who had designed both a college preparatory course and a general course.[5] Knowing that most of her students were not going on to college, Cooke wanted Dana Hall to go beyond making college preparation its only goal. The primary purpose of the school was:

> To help each girl to think, helping her to adjust to the disciplines of community living, exposing her to the best of her heritage and placing upon her the final responsibility of her own education.[6]

Emma Wilcox (left) on Grove Farm kitchen back step with Mabel Wilcox (right) by bath house in 1899.

According to Patricia Ruth Woodman Russell, Cooke herself took an active part in Wellesley's town civic and community affairs, and in 1912 she was a delegate at the National Convention of the Progressive Party. Cooke saw to it that the general course included advanced work in literature, languages, history, arts, and sciences. The preparatory and general courses were considered equally strong and "the same standard of scholarship will be required in each." Mabel's year-long course in art history—including trips to the Boston Public Library and Museum of Fine Arts—was "designed to give the student an acquaintance with masterpieces and a knowledge of the development of styles in architecture, sculpture and painting." A friend of notable artists, poets, and musicians of the day, Cooke also furnished each of the school's buildings with antique furnishings and artwork.

Mabel took courses in physics, German, and English in addition to art history. She saved her literature composition book, and one of her instructors graded some of her essays "creditable work," "excellent," "well considered," and "clearly and concisely told."[7]

Mabel was graduated in June, 1901, and her sister Etta wrote home to Grove Farm, "Mabel had a white K dress trimmed with lace and looked very sweet. She was well remembered in the way of presents. The pin from you and Papa, hatpin from Ralph, six Shaker boxes from Elsie, a pocket book from me, gold ring from Sarah. ..."[8] It is not certain what Mabel wanted to do after graduation. She could have attended Wellesley College with Elsie after Etta graduated, and Wellesley was probably what Emma and Sam hoped for Mabel. However, after spending the summer touring in Europe with Elsie, she chose not to enroll at Wellesley College. Her experiences at Dana Hall, with its non-collegiate orientation, may provide answers, or perhaps Mabel simply did not want to follow exactly in her sisters' footsteps. A more likely explanation would be that Mabel's interest in hospital nursing school was growing, perhaps stimulated by opportunities to learn more about the work of what today we call a registered nurse. Mabel also was thinking about training to be an architect. She'd say later, "I was always interested in architecture in a way. I didn't study it but I had thought maybe of going into architecture—before nursing." These two interests—nursing and architecture—found their way into her later career when she helped plan the tuberculosis sanatorium of Kauai, a Red Cross children's hospital in France and Kauai's first general hospital.

Though it is not known when exactly Mabel made her decision to enter the field of nursing, her desire to become a nurse and the inner discipline needed to undertake such a career were soon put to the test. Mabel recalled, "Mother didn't want me to be a nurse." A difficult dilemma for a young woman born to a family that valued its filial bonds. Emma had certain goals in mind for Etta, Elsie, and Mabel. Emma was intent upon preparing the girls for marriage after college. In a tightly knit, socially aware family such as the Wilcoxes on Kauai, the suitable prospects might be a plantation supervisor, a missionary descendent, a lawyer, or a physician. While Emma encouraged Etta's and Elsie's college education, she was opposed to the idea of her youngest daughter pursuing nurse's training. Mabel recalled, "She didn't want me to leave home; she thought nurses always got into difficulties." The image of nurses as servants with suspect morals was a popular one, and although Emma's experiences with home nurses were favorable, she probably would have agreed with Louisa May Alcott who wrote in her *Life, Letters and Journal*:

> Much trouble with nurses; have no idea of health, won't walk, sit over the fire and drink tea three times a day, ought to be intelligent, hearty set of women. Could do better myself, have to fill up all the deficiencies and do double duty.[9]

What happened next shows that Mabel's mother's wishes prevailed, at least for the time. In the fall of 1901, Mabel's parents arranged for

Wilcox family and friends by Grove Farm guest cottage in 1904. l to r: A.K.B. Lyman, Elsie, Sam, Charles (seated), Emma (seated), Gaylord, Lottie Jordan (seated), Anna Rice, Charlotte Mumford (seated), G.N., Mabel, and Ralph with dogs Carlo, Jocko, and Dewey.

her to remain East during Elsie's final year at Wellesley and study music in New York City. Mabel was close to some of her Dana Hall school friends in Orange, New Jersey, and though she must have been disappointed about her frustrated desire to pursue nursing as a career, she wrote home that "I am afraid I am cut out for a country jack although I think New York is just about right."[10]

Mabel was 19 when she and Elsie returned to Kauai together in 1902. Between youth and adulthood, she was at the stage of life where she felt old enough to make up her own mind about the future, and she still wanted to become a nurse. Not yet old enough to go to hospital training schools on the mainland, however, she continued to face disapproval from her mother.

Emma had no knowledge of hospital clinical training for graduate nurses, and she believed that medical science was a male profession. Her belief was not without cause: though the first hospital nursing schools were established in Europe and in the United States in the 1870s, a training school was not founded at Queen's Hospital until 1916. In the 1890s, the Queen's Hospital hired its first two trained nurses from Presbyterian Hospital in New York and Children's Hospital in San Francisco. Their duties were to "wait upon the patients, soothing them and applying their wants, [report] to the doctors and [carry] out their orders, do the cleaning of the building, the mending, sewing, and washing of the bedding and the table linen of the hospital and the clothing of the patients." The nursing world became better known in the 1880s with accounts of the Franciscan sisters at Kalaupapa on Molokai caring for lepers and helping Father Damien."[11] Fear of the disease and its danger to nurses also may have been behind some of Emma's worries about Mabel's future.

Dora Rice Isenberg, a Lihue friend of the Wilcox family and wife of the German Lutheran minister Hans Isenberg, took Mabel's side. She viewed nursing as respectable community service, and she reminded Emma that well-educated women in Europe and United States were being trained in nursing—and were becoming more independent of their mothers. Her advice to Emma was to "let her do what she wants to do."[12] Dora opened the way for Mabel, but Emma kept putting Mabel off. Hesitating, Emma finally imposed a condition intended to discourage her daughter and perhaps give more time to get her married: Mabel could enroll in nurse's school on the condition that she delay the start of her training for six more years, until she reached 25.

Mabel said later that she agreed "in a weak moment." Caught in the impasse of filial subordination and the strong desire to serve others—as well as new feelings of self-reliance, Mabel's dilemma seemed inevitable. She chose Johns Hopkins Hospital Training School for Nurses in Baltimore, and reconciled her domestic obligation by waiting six years. It was a compromise, but one that Mabel accepted, especially when she learned that Johns Hopkins did not enroll nursing students until they were 25. Looking back on the delay in getting started Mabel reflected, "Could have gone to college in between all that time I wasted, fooling around playing."[13]

Before they returned from the mainland, Etta, Elsie, and Mabel made plans to put an addition on the family beach house at Nawiliwili Bay. Soon after getting home, they began to stay at "Papalinahoa" and had their own steward and cook. As they entered adult Kauai society, the three sisters filled the weeks and months with the conventions of their time: swimming parties, dinners and dances, outings on horseback to Kukaua, Wailua Falls, and Kipukai, frequent teas at the home in Puhi of Uncle Albert and his wife; and long visits from such Honolulu friends as Belle Dickey and Ethel Damon. Ethel was attending Normal School at University of Hawaii after graduation from Punahou School before heading last to Wellesley College and Germany for additional study. Ethel remained Mabel and Elsie's close friend all of their lives. She was a writer, an historian and a linguist; serving during the First World War in France with Mabel as a Red Cross aide, secretary and translator.

While Elsie and Mabel were still on the mainland, Digby Sloggett, a Lihue Plantation supervisor and the son of a Honolulu physician courted Etta. When Elsie and Mabel returned, Etta and Digby announced their engagement. Etta was the first to marry and have children. Their brother Ralph, now his Uncle George's assistant at Grove Farm, and their childhood friend, Daisy Rice, also planned to be wed.

The Rices were gregarious and outgoing and the Wilcox boys liked the Rice girls because they were fun to be around, recalls Anna Scott Sloggett.[14] The social expectations of the two marriages prescribed routines for the family, from the engagement announcements to the ceremonies nearly a year later.

The Wilcox family applied itself to the tasks assigned to prospective brides, grooms, and bridesmaids, as well as the building and furnishing of two new houses for the betrothed couples nearby in Hanamaulu and at Grove Farm. Daisy Rice's brothers and other eligible bachelors on Kauai dated both Elsie and Mabel. Mabel was quiet with a quick sense of humor. Elsie and Mabel remained close to

Etta. With the birth of Richard Henry Sloggett in 1904, Elsie, Mabel, and their brothers visited Etta, Digby, and the baby nearly every day. When Etta developed a high fever a few weeks after giving birth, Elsie wrote, "An anxious day." They feared for Etta's life, though the next day Elsie wrote, "Etta still holding her own. ... Went to Etta's & spent day, taking care of the baby. Mother and Mabel came over in p.m. Ralph & Daisy down to spend the evening"[15] Etta recovered, and her health revived; Etta and Digby had five children.

With Etta married off and a mother herself, and Emma continuing to be in poor health, the responsibility for the direction of housekeeping was given to Elsie who found her days filled with dressmaking, baking, reading, and family entertainment. Elsie missed the intellectual camaraderie of Wellesley and wrote in her diary, "Served, Foreign mail, Heard from a lot of girls at College. Wish I could be there. Society news bad for us."[16] Elsie was more interested in current events than any of her brothers and Etta and Mabel. She attended political meetings on Kauai with her father, and later she and Mabel went to Honolulu with Sam and Emma for a legislative session. The sisterly bonds that tied Elsie and Mabel were strong, and in 1904 they made a four-month trip back to the mainland to visit Wilcox family in California and Lyman cousins in Illinois, as well as to attend a reunion of Elsie's Wellesley College class.

Back on Kauai in 1905, Elsie and Mabel helped found a women's civic and book club in Lihue. Among the other charter members were their mother, sister Etta, and sister-in-law Daisy. Like other contemporary women's clubs on the mainland, the Mokihana Club served as a means for women with many interests to meet with other women, and later, to further women-centered issues.[17]

Mabel grew close to her Uncle George around Grove Farm and took an interest in the Lihue Hospital and its care of patients. She, like others, probably learned of problems with Richard J. Wilkinson, M.D., an Irish physician then in charge of both the Lihue and Makaweli plantation hospitals. Wilkinson drew severe criticism for his indifference to plantation families with sick children, and after several years he was given notice. Hans Isenberg commented,

Dr. Wilkinson has made himself more and more disliked. Twice I have had to warn him when he flatly refused to obey the urgent call of an anxious father to see a very sick child, although he had ample time. The second time ... when he refused to see a sick baby and the baby died, I had to call him by order of the Directors, that he would lose his position if this happened again. Now lately he has done the same thing and the Directors have felt it their duty to protect their people from further painful experiences.[18]

One wonders if witnessing these early experiences with plantation doctors imprinted Mabel Wilcox with the importance of sensitivity and empathy in public health. Her determination to go away to hospital nursing training held steady, and she enrolled in a home-study general course offered by the Chautauqua Correspondence School of Nursing in preparation for her training. Over a period of six months at Grove Farm, she studied introductory lectures mailed weekly from New York and successfully took written tests in Principles of Nursing, Anatomy, Sick-Room Management, Diet, Materia Medica, Bacteriology and Diseases. She also learned about the possibilities of nurse's work: private duty then being the most common type of employment, which involved caring for a single patient at home or in a hospital; visiting nursing, part of the growing public health movement; and hospital nursing which focused on ward work.[19] After the long wait, Mabel would begin her hospital training and learn firsthand about nursing's authority, mission, and its changing roles in the early twentieth century.

Chapter Four

"A MODEL OF ITS KIND"

Mabel's formal education at Johns Hopkins Hospital Training School in Baltimore gave her an even stronger sense of commitment by preparing her with the technical skills of applied science, and introducing her to clinical medicine, theories of disease, and the social and economic issues crucial to modern health care. Johns Hopkins Hospital was a lasting influence in her life, and her experiences strengthened her receptivity to the suffering of others and confirmed her sense of community service—both of which would inform her long nursing career on Kauai.

Mabel was the first person from Hawaii to be selected by Johns Hopkins Hospital Training School when she was accepted for the spring term in 1908. As one of America's foremost training institutions, it selected a class every year of about 40 "pupil nurses" who entered the three-year program of academic courses, laboratory work, and hospital ward service.[1]

"My first application was turned down," she recalled. "Little *kamaaina* from Kauai, they never heard of any such place. They turned me down ... I [had] just got a hold of people here, the doctor, the minister, so then I went to Dr. Judd because he was well known right away." James R. Judd, M.D.—the Honolulu surgeon, grandson of missionary physician Gerrit P. Judd, friend of Albert and Emma Wilcox and one of the founders of Kauikeolani Children's Hospital—was a recent graduate of Yale and Columbia University Medical School.[2] He was the one who helped Mabel gain admission.

In the months before she left Kauai, she learned to drive Uncle George's automobile, one of the first on the island. Mabel was also dating Philip Rice, Daisy's brother, and Charles Dole, the First District

Magistrate of the County of Kauai. She saw both frequently, noting in her diary, "Philip and I went to the races in Kapaa. The two troublesome tires have been off and on 18 times … Drove Father to Koloa in A.M … over in 45 min. and back in 1 hour … Philip to call in evening, wanted to go driving but I would not go." Mabel and Philip had alarmed her family a few weeks earlier: "Went for a drive with Philip—to Wailua and over wood-road to Kilohana, bad road so late in getting home." And, lest he feel left out, Mabel "played golf for first time on new course" with Charles, Elsie, and Bessie Rice, probably at Wailua.[3]

When the time came for Mabel to leave for Baltimore, Dora Isenberg and Aunt Emma Wilcox gave lunch parties for her. She wrote: "Packed in A.M. Took mother to Papalinahoa in auto. Etta, Digby & children, Elsie and I left for Honolulu. Had quite a send off."

After a week's stay on Oahu, Mabel, with Etta, Digby and their children, sailed for San Francisco where they visited Wilcox cousins and friends in San Francisco, Oakland and San Rafael. Mabel recorded a bit of uncharacteristic chitchat in her diary, perhaps reflective of her excitement:

[H]eard a little romance from "Ouija" after six months at J.H. Hospital I will meet Dr. John Monroe, tall, handsome, light and well-established. Engaged to him in two years—married in S.F.

Leaving for San Francisco – Digby Sloggett, Etta, Mabel, with Sloggett children, Margaret and Richard.

before completing my course—will live in N.Y. and then home. Elsie will visit me in N.Y. and meet lawyer of unknown name who is not wealthy but smart and thus meet her fate.[4]

This imagined scenario was matched by a real but less desirable incident in San Francisco that brought out Mabel's anxiety about the future. Introduced to a San Francisco physician with whom she attended a piano recital, Mabel later went out with him again. She wrote in her diary:

> Went to the "Fairmont" to dinner with Dr. Connell. Good dinner and a beautiful hotel ... However, I was bored to death by the Dr. after dinner, which took about three hours we wandered over the hotel hunting for empty rooms!! Then started home—our car went to Presidio Ave. so the Dr. suggested we walk the remaining four blocks. I repented shortly for he began to persuade me to give up my course on the plea of my strength and then on the plea of family life being preferable. Ha! Ha! I was very decided in my answer but he was so sure I didn't know my mind and wants to see me again. Not on your life.[5]

Mabel arrived at Johns Hopkins Hospital ready to start her career. It was a period of important change in the history of American medical and nursing education, as well as reform in the day-to-day workings of hospitals. As medical historian Charles Rosenberg has written, "Intellectual content was to be made more demanding while as a necessary prerequisite, hours of ward work were to be curtailed and the course lengthened from two to three years."[6] Johns Hopkins Hospital already had gained an international reputation in the 20 years that it had been open, and as a teaching hospital it had been envisioned as "a model of its kind." The hospital offered large facilities for patient care, one of the finest medical school faculties and house staff in the United States, and good financial resources.

The nurses' training school attracted nurse-educators who had a broad vision of the needs of nursing services in clinical medicine, public health, and preventive care. The interdependence of clinical treatment and outpatient care turned out to be one of the progressive lessons Mabel learned at Johns Hopkins. It was the important legacy of prominent nursing education leaders: Isabel Hampton was the Hopkins nursing school principal from 1889 to 1894; her successor, Adelaide Nutting, served from 1894 to 1906.[7]

The longer training curriculum, introduced before Mabel was enrolled, included new laboratory courses and programs in dietetics and psychiatry. Moreover, the nursing school principals at Johns Hopkins Hospital were in charge of all of the nurses in the hospital. The nurse educators thus had potent influence in the creation of ward routines, avoiding waste and controlling costs, keeping discipline among the patients, and fostering cooperation by the house staff. Medical school professors like William Osler, William Welch, William Halstead, Howard Kelly and Harvey Cushing were teaching medical students and residents, working beside them with hospital nursing students in cases involving internal medicine, surgery, obstetrics, and gynecology. Kenneth Ludmerer, M.D., in *Learning to Heal: The Development of American Medical Education* describes the significance of Johns Hopkins Medical School as an elite institution:

> From the very start, Johns Hopkins was a radical departure in medical education. Students were carefully selected, with the bachelor's degree a prerequisite for admission. Classes were small and students frequently tested and evaluated. Two years' instruction were provided in the basic sciences, with extensive

Mabel (in back row) with Johns Hopkins Hospital nursing school classmates c. 1910. Students pose with "Charlie Brown" (skeleton) "Oh my weren't we reprimanded for that, taking 'Charlie Brown' out the window, and posing – then they locked it in – kept door locked so we couldn't get in the room where he was kept," Mabel later recalled.

laboratory work mandatory for every student, and two years of rigorous training were also provided in the clinical subjects, with the students gaining experience at the hospital bedside. A true university spirit pervaded the school, for it viewed research as one of its primary missions, and it strove to train investigators and teachers of medicine as well as practitioners.[8]

Mabel and her classmates were housed in the nursing school residence next to the hospital: a homey dormitory offering the single women of Johns Hopkins a place to live in the city. From there they launched into six months' probationary training, a preliminary period which began with Mabel's remark that "none of us ever hoped that we would be able to give a sweat bath, a typhoid tub, or live through months of harrowing night duty." The "probs," as they were called, were kept off hospital wards for five or six months. Their mornings were spent in a diet kitchen; their afternoons given to lectures and demonstrations in anatomy, physiology, practical nursing, hygiene and materia medica. About Florence R. Sabin, M.D., a recent graduate of the Johns Hopkins medical school and an associate professor of anatomy, Mabel wrote:

> Dog day with Dr. Sabin. Very interesting—saw muscles of the abdomen, legs and shoulders ... Dr. Sabin lecture on Evolution. Very difficult ... Dr. Sabin demonstration—digestive organs of dog. *Very* interesting ... Exam in Physiology and Anatomy. Fair Exam. I had the vertebrae.[9]

In July 1908 she completed probationary work, standing respectably at third in her class, and was accepted as a "junior." "Put on my blue and was fitted to a cap," Mabel wrote. Her class history later noted, "The transition from the state of probationers to that of accepted nurses was of monumentous [sic] importance to every one of us. We were assigned to duty in different wards, and soon fell into the busy life." In addition to eight hours daily in ward labor, Mabel spent 30 hours a week in lecture room work and preparation. Her diary gives a firsthand picture of the discipline of training, as well as Mabel's compassion and growing knowledge.

> Very ill child in clinic. Mother would go behind screen and cry so child would not see her. Very pathetic ... Taken from Children's Clinic. In Operating Room and Woman's Surgical—In one *operation* handed sponges & never felt more awkward in my life ... Still in Operating Room. Shaved a man's hand ... Bandaged a woman's foot. Saw a syphalitic [sic]. ... Sent to Ward G. Scrubbed and made

beds. 7–12 & 4–7 ... Given the Nursery with Mrs. Shiff. Four children. Cases: nephrites [sic]; broken femur; osteomyelitis. Feel very stumped and slow ... Mabel Hall the little girl who came into Phipps on July 24th is one of my patients. Has endocarditis and is very miserable ... Mabel Hall developed diphtheria—Miss Cheney and I had to go to [Ward I] and clean up and have anti-toxin. Off the ward for 2 hours. Baby Price, burn case, died meanwhile. Hard day on G ... Had my thumb opened for infection. Very painful ... Finger very painful—opened again—cut to the bone ... Glad to be off duty as I was about at the end of my rope—feel too tired to move and have felt so for several weeks.[10]

Busy to the point of exhaustion, Mabel chose a passage from Charles Dickens' *David Copperfield* to reassure herself: "My advice to you is to cheer up, to keep a good heart, and to know your own value." She passed her twenty-sixth birthday and wrote "Did not celebrate my birthday as I am still 7–7 and am ready for bed after supper. No one knows it was my birthday. Last year I was in Shanghai."

Mabel often heard from home, but she did not see her parents and sister again until they met on the East Coast in 1909. She received permission from Georgina Ross, R.N., the school's superintendent, for a leave "to meet Papa, Mama and Elsie in N.Y." Mabel took a train to New York City and "surprised them by my arrival."[11] Elsie was about to start a tour of Egypt, Palestine, and other parts of the Middle East, followed by a long stay in Berlin where she studied German, French, and music.

At Grove Farm, Wilcox family life saw Ralph and Daisy living close by as Ralph was given more plantation and business responsibilities by his uncle. Etta, Digby, and their three children had moved to Maui, but Charles Wilcox was at Koloa Plantation where he was promoted to plantation manager in April 1909. That summer Charles married Marion Waterhouse. Some months before, Gaylord was married to Ethel Kulamanu Mahelona Wilcox, the adopted child of Uncle Albert.[12] Gaylord became head overseer of Koloa Plantation when his brother stepped up that year. An informal outdoor group photograph at Grove Farm shows Ralph and Daisy, Charles and Gaylord and their new wives, Etta and Digby, and three of the Sloggett grandchildren, Richard, Margaret, and Dorothea, along with Sam and Emma Wilcox. Mabel and Elsie were thousands of miles away.

Still, life in Baltimore had its own rewards. Mabel was gaining experience. In the crowded days and nights of hospital duty at

Johns Hopkins Mabel learned how to observe and treat patients in public wards and in private care rooms. She became interested in surgical cases and attended patients with "kidney trouble, spinal trouble, broken leg, gallstones, excision neck gland and tumor." Working with her professors, too, was training in itself. The full-time medical school professors shaped the clinical experience of hospital "pupil nurses," sometimes in memorable ways. Mabel described an incident involving herself and Harvey Cushing, M.D., the pioneer in neurosurgery. Mabel recalled:

> He cussed me out in the operating room. I asked to get a little more general surgery than he was giving. It was most interesting because he was doing wonderful work and a wonderful surgeon, but I wasn't getting general surgery. He really was a very nice person. Of course he was under terrific strain at that time, brain surgery was just starting. When he bawled me out, I hadn't done anything wrong. He came back later and apologized and said he had made a mistake.[13]

Pressures of training were always on her mind, particularly after the resignation of the training school's superintendent in 1910. Mabel saved a clipping in her diary that stated that Georgina Ross had suffered from a "serious nervous collapse, due it is reported, to overwork in the performance of her duties at the hospital."[14] Tired and under stress herself, Mabel's 1910 diary consists of all blank pages when she went on night duty. Later, she noted, "Still night duty ... Might as well be buried." She had experienced one of the oldest paradoxes in modern medical education—a hospital claims to provide an excellent environment for learning while systematically depriving its students of sleep.[15]

When Mabel and her classmates became seniors—the milestone in their training—their class book noted, "This new dignity brought with it added responsibilities. Those who were put in charge of wards say that the sensation of waking up in the morning to find themselves 'famous' was indescribable."[16] Seniors were taught to take more problems into their own hands and solve them.

Baltimore was a racially segregated city; in the hospital's public wards, African-American patients were treated apart from others. Mortality among "coloreds," as they were called, was twice as high as among Caucasian patients, and work in these wards was particularly difficult although Mabel did comment on their predicament "[I] feel more and more hopeless about the place," she wrote of wards in general. She broke a mirror while making rounds with a resident and wrote of her troubles: "Sure sign of bad luck. About 12 was [sic] sent to front office—there I was told I was to have charge of Ward M [one of the public wards]. Really don't know how I can do it."[17] When a dangerous diphtheria epidemic broke out in the wards from February to March 1911, the students and other nurses' discipline, cooperation, and self control were tested even further as they took thousands of throat cultures. Some nurses even had to be confined to Ward G, used for isolation. The student magazine reported, "The spirit with which the affected wards accepted the enforced quarantine presented an interesting study. Some arrived gaily, suitcase in hand, as if on a pleasure bent; others came, with pillow and blanket, gratefully glad of the unexpected rest; a few were afraid that the shades of former patients would trouble their dreams, and hesitated on the threshold."[18]

At the end, the hard work was worth it. When Mabel graduated, she had completed courses that included physiology, surgery, and clinical disease. Her Certificate of Professional Training shows that her grades averaged 88.5 points, a solid record. Amazingly, Mabel found time to work on the Johns Hopkins Hospital Training School senior class magazine, *J.H.H.T.S.*, the first publication of its kind at the school. She also had attended special lectures on the history of nursing and such social issues as public health and the women's suffrage movement. One of the school speakers was Isabel Stewart, R.N., who gave a talk on the new graduate program in nursing and health management at Teachers' College at Columbia. The class magazine reported:

> We were most interested in hearing of the department of social and district work, and our interest has been kept up by unusual opportunities of hearing the work discussed in our own classroom by many settlement and district workers. Some of us have already planned to enter that field and are hopeful that an opportunity may come to enjoy the course in Teachers' College later on.[19]

With graduation from Hopkins in 1911, Mabel enrolled in the American Red Cross, considered at that time the unofficial reserve of the U.S. Army Nurses Corps. She did not know then that only a few years later she would participate briefly in the Columbia program while awaiting an overseas Red Cross nursing assignment during the First World War—or, as a further coincidence, that she would be assigned to a Johns Hopkins Medical School Red Cross pediatrician in wartime Le Havre, France.

The training Mabel received at Johns Hopkins Hospital was impressive in its thoroughness and breadth, preparing her for both clinical nursing and public health work. Too, the school fostered a strong sense of potentiality among women—an orientation that would serve Mabel well in her years in the male-dominated world of plantation Hawaii. Elsie Lawler, R.N., who became superintendent in 1910, was a graduate of the school a dozen years earlier. Lawler was "a strong, friendly and conscientious person who got along well with doctors, patients, nurses and students."[20]

When commencement came in May 1911, it was a time to forget self-discipline and enjoy the "realizm [sic] and idealism" of their experience. Students lampooned one another's foibles and follies in the class magazine, using nicknames to protect the innocent. Mabel's was "Bill." One entry asked, "Wouldn't you like to see 'Billy' uncork?"—perhaps an allusion to Mabel's characteristic reserve. Joining the fun, Mabel wrote prophecies for 16 members of her class, including her own. Her predictions followed the many unromantic months at nursing school. In what reads like a satire, romance is allowed in, but only to be mocked away.

PROPHECY OF THE PROPHET

I saw my classmate, Billy Wilcox, reading a mysterious looking book entitled "Notes on Class of 1911." Bill looked so queer that I did not dare to speak, but crawled under the table. But I noted that as the book disappeared from her hand as by magic, a small piece of paper fluttered to the floor. Bill did not see this, but tip-toed out of the room as if spellbound.

I was much frightened, but reached out and got this slip of paper, and to my astonishment it read:

"Miss Wilcox, globe trotter, has settled down for a short time to add a few improvements to a new field of work, which she originally discovered. Through this marvelous discovery, by various impressions, shades and lights, Bill is able to tell the exact condition of the heart when in love. Her further studies reveal the details." Doesn't it seem strange that our Bill should be doing such work? [21]

A photograph of Mabel's class shows them at Johns Hopkins. In the coming years two thirds of the graduates entered into long nursing careers: their histories show that a dozen of them eventually became hospital head nurses; nine members of the class, including Mabel, went into tuberculosis and maternal child health care; two more graduates specialized in psychiatric nursing; and two more became missionary nurses in India and Newfoundland. And, "Prophecy of the Prophet" notwithstanding, the hospital training school archives also show that 12 graduates of the class did indeed marry.[22]

As a graduate of one of the leading American hospital schools, Mabel was one of a rapidly growing number of women who were in possession of the skills needed for the "new nursing." Mabel's future organizational life reaffirmed that the success of improved health care in the early twentieth century depended greatly on the closeness of professionally trained women to individual patients and families. Johns Hopkins had taught her that the new nursing was a profession. As Susan Reverby, the social historian, has written in *Ordered to Care,* leaders in nursing education "saw science as a gender-free zone that could transform the content of their work and the status of their field."[23] Mabel's diary entries from 1908 to 1911 suggest what others have said: a hospital like Johns Hopkins was "a School, workplace and home combined, where student nurses, separated from their homes and families, took their place in the world of female authority."[24]

Mabel's rigorous training experience and her care of sick patients of all ages and ethnicities at Johns Hopkins had made her fully aware of the collective purposes of preventive and clinical medicine. The rigorous and stimulating world of the teaching hospital prepared her for a demanding role on Kauai where she tackled one concrete problem after another: controlling an infectious, killer disease like tuberculosis; helping lower infant mortality; and becoming a catalyst for new clinical facilities on the island—a public sanatorium and an independent general hospital. It was on the job visiting men, women, and children

Mabel Wilcox's Johns Hopkins Hospital Nursing School graduating class. Mabel in back row, fifth from the left.

in Kauai's sugar plantation camps and in more remote, scattered rural areas that Mabel learned about her community's health care problems, the uncertainties of everyday life on an isolated agricultural island, and unpredictable medical services. It was also back home that she personally learned to cope with her family's tragedies—sad events that drew her family even nearer to one another.

Mabel's Johns Hopkins Hospital nursing pin and nursing cape.

PART II 1912–1929

Chapter Five

WILIKOKI: KAUKA WAHINE

When Mabel returned to Kauai from Baltimore her leisure time activities consisted largely of visiting with relatives and friends. Framed in a family context, she nursed Charles and Marion's son Sam through an illness, in addition to going to Honolulu with Marion to be her private-duty nurse after hospital surgery. In March 1912, Mabel and her parents left for a four-month trip to Louisiana, Florida, North Carolina, Maryland, and New York, where they met Elsie as she returned from her studies and travel in Europe. Mabel stopped off to be with some of her former Johns Hopkins Hospital classmates in Baltimore for three weeks and even received an offer there to take a tuberculosis nursing position at the Mt. Wilson Hospital in the city.

She chose to return to Hawaii with Sam, Emma, and Elsie, however, and was hired as a school nurse at Kawaiahao Seminary in Honolulu. Back on Kauai, Elsie continued to expand her interests outside home life, developing her capacities in community affairs. She was elected president of the Mokihana Club for a second time; there were now over 40 members who took a growing interest, through study groups and lectures, in Hawaii's public schooling and social welfare needs. The Mokihana Club reminds one of what historian Anne Firor Scott has written about other American women's associations of the time: "Consequences of community life went in tandem with consequences for the women themselves."[1]

At Grove Farm, G. N. was making plans for a two-story addition to the old house. He wanted to continue to use the one-story plantation house, which he considered historical, and received suggestions from two different Honolulu architects for designs. Then 74 years old—Sam and Emma were in their 60s—G. N. would later say that "the house was for his children," his unmarried nieces, Mabel and Elsie.

Then in July 1913 the unexpected and tragic occurred: Ralph Wilcox accidentally drowned swimming at Haena on Kauai's northern shore. The family was devastated by the event, Ralph's death causing deep sorrow and a sense of futility. Everyone at Grove Farm was desolate, and recovery came very slowly.

To help console Daisy and fill her loss, sister Mary Rice Scott offered her youngest daughter for Daisy to raise and adopt. G. N. asked Ralph's younger brother Charles to give up his position as manager of Koloa Plantation to take Ralph's place at Grove Farm Company, and a house was built for Charles and Marion at Grove Farm. Mabel returned from Honolulu, and she and Elsie, Charles and Marion and their young children tried to supply what was now missing in the social life of their widowed sister-in-law, their older parents, and uncle.[2]

Mabel applied for and received the newly created position of Territorial tuberculosis nurse for Kauai when it became available, and she received the appointment and began to work on Kauai in October of 1913. The Bureau of Tuberculosis had been established in 1910 for the prevention and control of the infectious disease. As such, Mabel's first public health duties were part of the Territorial Board of Health's new visiting nurses service and "anti-tuberculosis campaign."

Tuberculosis is a chronic, airborne bacterial infection that usually strikes the lungs and is marked by continuous physiological misery for the sick. The symptoms are a persistent fever, coughing, blood in the sputum, and weight loss. Tuberculosis was the major health problem in the Islands in the early twentieth century, and it was the leading cause of death in both Hawaii and on the mainland.

Bacteriology revolutionized medicine and public health in the late nineteenth century when the role of microscopic pathogenic organisms was defined. A modern clinical diagnosis of the infection was possible with the isolation of the bacillus by Robert Koch as the cause of tuberculosis. Hygienic laboratories were established by health departments and helped to convince the medical profession that tuberculosis was a communicable disease. By 1910 (the year Hawaii's Bureau of Tuberculosis was established), according to public health historian John Duffy, "Most states had made the reporting of tuberculosis and other communicable diseases compulsory."[3] With growing acceptance of the germ theory of diseases and discovery of the causative organisms of tuberculosis there was a professional and public demand for the care of persons ill with tuberculosis.

The Territorial public health "anti-tuberculosis campaign" was established because of the blunt fact that Hawaii had a tuberculosis death rate greater than most American states. Archibald N. Sinclair, M.D., the supervisor of the Territory's program, led educational efforts to arouse interest in case finding to halt the spread of the disease. In 1905, Sinclair reminded Hawaii Medical Society members that "Tuberculosis Pulmonalia is the most disease that the medical practitioner has to deal with, not alone on account of the vital importance it has for the patient affected, but also on account of the great menace to public health every case of this disease must be."[4] On Kauai Sinclair wrote articles in the *Garden Island* and enlisted the support of ministers and others against the spread of the disease before Mabel's appointment as visiting nurse.

As such, there was much to be done by the tuberculosis nurse on the plantations and in other rural districts. Writing to Mabel about her new work, Archibald Sinclair emphasized the urgency of finding active pulmonary cases and locating carriers of the disease. He wrote Mabel that she must be prepared to investigate all suspicious cases, give sputum examinations, and forward specimen samples to a government physician while creating basic records for every case. Sinclair told her that a major problem was Kauai's plantation physicians, noting that her duties would consist of "visiting cases of tuberculosis reported by private physicians … which they do not care to supervise or assume the responsibility of avoiding infection of others."[5]

It was a large and challenging job, especially compared to her duties at Kawaiahao. Mabel crisscrossed the island, making home visits to search out the unusually tenacious disease and talking with infected, highly contagious persons. In so doing, she mapped a largely uncharted public health terrain and got to know the residents of Kauai well. She worked alone most of the time, or with her father. It was hard, dangerous work. "It was long, slow, uphill work," Mabel said. "[S]ometimes I thought I wasn't accomplishing much." In particular, she assisted Hawaiian families in their travails.

A typical case? Well, we'd go to a house where we knew there was a case. We'd try to get them to live better, not expose the rest of the family. Actually, there was little we could do except keep them from eating out of a common poi bowl if possible, tell them not to sleep together, be careful not to cough in someone's face. I used to take my father. He helped me a lot (he was retired by this time). The Hawaiians liked and respected him. He spoke Hawaiian. He was my chief assistant.[6]

She was called *Wilikoki*, Wilcox in Hawaiian, and *Kauka Wahine*, woman doctor or nurse. Mabel instructed the families how to separate infants and children from those who were infected, showed them how to disinfect clothing and bedding, and explained reasons for using clean eating utensils and dishes.

Looking back on her first few years of nursing on Kauai, Mabel recalled that she had been given a list of 71 tuberculosis cases "scattered from one end of the island to another." She found that "many of these were dead, had moved away, or apparently had never existed, while there were numbers of cases which had been reported but never recorded."[7] Her search revealed 31 cases and another 32 not under supervision of any kind. A year later her total was 89, and by 1915 it had grown to 111 cases. "This is a steady increase of cases," she noted, "but a great majority now are incipient whereas formerly they were well-advanced, hopeless cases."

Mabel added her observations of the extensive local superstitions about tuberculosis, as well as notes on what she considered the general ignorance and carelessness about the disease. She confronted many incorrect theories, but foremost among these was the popular belief that tuberculosis was invariably fatal. She observed:

> The mother who assures me there is no need for her to safeguard herself and the younger children because her older son's illness is Divinely sent … The Christian Scientist who does not care to take any precautionary measures because he is not told to in Science & Health … and the man who is both physically and mentally blind insisted on sleeping with his children in an air tight room.[8]

At the same time, she tried not to judge. When she encountered Hawaiian medicinal practices, she said that "I didn't feel I should disturb them because they believed so implicitly in them." "I let them go ahead," she added. "I told them what I thought and what I thought they should do, my way of thinking, but I didn't try to disturb their beliefs." Of all of her frustrations, however, what stood out were the people she met who believed tuberculosis was hereditary or a nervous disorder. Their attitude often made prevention impossible, as many cases went unreported because of the assumption that the illness was unavoidable. As Mark Caldwell states in *The Last Crusade*, the diagnosis of tuberculosis appeared to condemn the infected to an agonizing end.[9]

Mabel kept basic field service records, supplies, and a growing nursing library in the former family schoolhouse cottage at Grove Farm.

This was the first public health office on Kauai, and it gave her a space of her own to consult such works as Ella La Motte's, *The Tuberculosis Nurse*, S. Adolphus Knopf's, *Tuberculosis: A Preventable and Curable Disease*, F. R. Walter's, *Sanatoria for Consumptives*, and other books that she acquired at nursing school or ordered from the mainland.

It wasn't just home visits and educational work that Mabel became involved with, in her capacity as Territorial tuberculosis nurse. The Territory's tuberculosis campaign recognized that overcrowded and unsanitary housing conditions on plantations as well as in the more remote districts compounded the problem of the communicability of tuberculosis and other infectious diseases. Palama Settlement, the private social welfare agency in Honolulu, took the lead in drawing the Territory's attention to tenement housing conditions and associated health problems. In 1912 Palama Settlement presented a "Public Welfare Exhibit" in Kalihi as part of the anti-tuberculosis campaign. The agency also opened a model cottage and contrasted it with unhealthy housing conditions, highlighting needed changes in sanitation and the replacement of inadequate plantation labor camp barracks. Such educational exhibits had started on the mainland, beginning in Baltimore in 1904.[10]

The scientist Rene Dubois, in his work *Mirage of Health*, draws attention to the relationship of epidemics like tuberculosis to the Industrial Revolution and the uprooted cultural, social, and economic lives of labor migrations. In Hawaii the disease first had spread in the nineteenth century because of the lack of immunity of Hawaiians. Later it was coupled with the poor living conditions of the plantations' imported contract labor. But Dubois also said,

> In any given country the death rates of infections are liable to soar to a high peak shortly after the shift from a rural to an industrial type of economy; then the epidemics lose their acute character and their mortality falls as prosperity becomes more widespread.[11]

Measured by the decline in mortality from tuberculosis from 1910 to World War II, this is what seems to have occurred in Hawaii and the mainland. First there was the cyclical and self-limiting nature of the disease as mortality from tuberculosis began to fall gradually in the mid-nineteenth century. Second there was the demand for appropriate facilities to isolate those infected by the disease. The possibility of a tuberculosis cure was a daunting problem in the early twentieth century, but segregated bed rest, managed diet, and lung surgery were remedies, if not complete relief from the disease.

To give specialized care to those afflicted, and to protect healthy persons from further exposure and danger of infection, there were nearly 400 tuberculosis hospitals, or sanatoria, in the United States by 1910 providing a rest cure, managed diet, schooling, and outdoor work. Two Hawaii sanatoria, Leahi Home in Honolulu and the Maui County Farm and Sanatorium in Kula had been built, and in addition to her home visits, Mabel was soon involved in helping plan a tuberculosis hospital for Kauai.

Mabel said that she had started thinking about the design and operation of a sanatorium soon after she took up her Kauai nursing duties. She said that "it became apparent from the start that a patient learned more in a day in a hospital than from many house visits ... the plantation hospitals were inadequate both in equipment and space, so a plea was made for the erection of a special Tuberculosis Hospital ... the response from the Drs., planters & others was most gratifying."[12]

Oil portrait of Samuel Mahelona by Lloyd L. Sexton, 1955, which hangs in the lobby of Samuel Mahelona Memorial Hospital

Mabel used her scientific training, the practical experience of her fieldwork on Kauai, her participation in the Mokihana Club, and a planning trip to mainland hospitals and sanatoria to study the program needs for the new facility. Like Elsie, Mabel had been elected president of the Mokihana Club, just as the club was turning its attention to subjects of public health. Mabel described the field of tuberculosis nursing and her ideas for the sanatoria in a talk to the club in 1916. Her family gave her their full support; in fact, they were at the center of her ambitious planning. According to Mary Cooke, who interviewed Mabel many years later, "Kauai got its TB hospital after Miss Mabel talked with Uncle Albert and Aunt Emma." Albert and Emma knew tuberculosis from the inside because Emma's son, Samuel Mahelona, had died from the disease several years earlier. They told Mabel that they would donate the sum of $25,000 for a sanatorium building under two conditions: none of the gift was to be spent for land, and the hospital was to be a memorial to Samuel Mahelona.[13] It was another example of the Wilcox family's growing involvement in health care reform.

During her trip to the mainland, Mabel observed settlement house work in Boston and medical social services at the Massachusetts General Hospital and Boston Dispensary. She also visited the Jefferson Hospital in Philadelphia and Johns Hopkins Hospital. On her way back to Honolulu she called on Philip K. Brown, M.D., at his newly opened Arequipa Sanatorium in Fairfax, California. The small hospital was for the "treatment of early cases of tuberculosis in wage earning women." Aware of the problems of the isolation of patients she saw there, Mabel said after her trip:

Connected with it is a Pottery where the patients as soon as able may work and earn according to the amount of work they are able to do. Some of the girls become very clever and earn as much as $3 a day, which is considerable as the working day never exceeds 5 hours even for the physically ablest of the patients. This wage earning is a solution to one of the greatest problems of sanatoriums. Patients when they are convalescent become restless, discouraged, or mentally disturbed over financial conditions long before they are physically fit to go to work, but if in some way they may become wage earners, even tho it may be on a small scale, they may become contented once more & willing to prolong their necessary rest. With our new tuberculosis Hosp. we hope to find employment for our convalescents on the grounds of the farm & if possible pay them according to the am't of work they do.[14]

She brought an Arts and Crafts style vase home from Arequipa home. On Kauai, her field work and studies showed that at least 40 infected persons were in need of sanatorium treatment. Mabel worked up cost estimates in consultation with plantation physicians, and in February 1915, these figures were presented to the Kauai Planters' Association "with the idea of securing from the plantations, and the public, funds for the construction of the hospital." The Planters' Association invited Sinclair to look over possible hospital sites, and he recommended a plateau above Kapaa on the windward side of the island. The property was public land, 120 acres in size, and it was soon set aside by the Territorial legislature. The acreage was large enough for the development of the hospital, as well as a farm and dairy to provide vegetables, eggs, milk, meat, and poultry for the patients.[15]

The Kauai County Board of Supervisors next made a commitment to maintain the proposed facility by annual appropriations, and, with the promise of the public land, County funds, and the matching gift from Albert and Emma Wilcox, plans moved ahead rapidly. Mabel prepared the building program for four well-ventilated, small wards and six individual rooms. An X-Ray room, operating room, dispensary, tray room, and kitchen were also included in the plan. Mabel's emphasis was on domestic architecture, with broad *lanais* to serve as open-air connecting hallways. Describing the sanatorium design, Mabel wrote

It is planned for 30 patients but the large verandas allow for more at the start if necessary. However, with the present high cost of building we may not be able to equip entirely for that number. One branch of work I had hoped to install was the care & treatment of children suffering from tubercular glands or bone diseases. With an X-Ray, operating rooms, good food, sunlight, sea air, what ideal conditions and what a chance for results. But the Board of Health does not allow an appropriation for the care of such non-contagious cases & the County will have considerable initial expenses, so this would have to be done by private subscription for equipment and endowment.

We hope to make this hospital not just an institution for the care of a contagious disease, but an instructive center where patients may learn the care of themselves & the protection of others. We want to make it a house rather than a hospital, a park rather than a dreary isolation camp. And we want the interest of the community to encourage one & all to make it such.[16]

The Honolulu architect Clinton B. Ripley was hired by the County to prepare the building specifications and working drawings. Ripley recently had been the architect for the Kauai County building, and he had been selected by G. N. to design the Grove Farm house addition. Mabel was appointed Mahelona's first general manager. This appointment was a first of its kind for a woman in Hawaii.[17]

Samuel Mahelona Memorial Hospital was built on a bluff above Kapaa in 1917 and enlarged in 1925, for the treatment of Kauai's tuberculosis patients. Mabel planned the sanatorium operations and ordered all the equipment and other furnishings. (Photo ourtesy the Hawaii State Archives.)

Chapter Six

KAUAI'S MOTHERS AND INFANTS

Through her tuberculosis nursing on Kauai, Mabel developed familiarity with the health care needs of Kauai's main population: Hawaiians, Chinese, Portuguese, Japanese, Koreans and Filipinos. She gained first hand knowledge of the circumstances, conventions, and constraints of class, race, and gender, and her everyday experiences reinforced what she had learned about public health at Johns Hopkins. She understood that numerous things contributed to health: science, education, personal behavior, income, nutrition, housing, cultural traditions, and increased access to medical care

Her sensitivity to cultural traditions was recalled later by one of Kauai's *kupuna*, Gabriel I, who lived near Grove Farm as a child:

> I remember [her] as a nurse with the Department of Health when she would make regular visits to the area, especially in Nawiliwili. She'd stop at one house to find out how the families are, the children. Come to our place, the same thing, would visit with my mother, say 'How are the children? Any problems?' and my mother would say 'No.' and she would go on up the valley. So she really spent a lot of time making house to house visits. This was something that the Hawaiian families couldn't forget.[1]

Mabel realized that these exchanges were vital. As she said in 1916:

> The public health nurse who has established confidence in the house by follow-up work of one sort or another, and who is rendering service in the house can secure a hearing which no one else can, & with her knowledge of disease and the necessity for sanitation can readily instill the principles of prevention.[2]

During the early part of the 1900s, the Territory had no maternal and child health nursing program. As the Kauai tuberculosis visiting nurse, however, Mabel directed her practical efforts towards mothers and infants as well. The reason was obvious: Infant mortality was commonplace. Young immigrant mothers on plantations, separated from their homeland families and home birthing customs, were still inexperienced in pre-natal and post-natal care. They and their newborns faced the hazards of unsanitary plantation living conditions, various grades of malnutrition, and infections like diarrhea, pneumonia, and tuberculosis. Nearly one of every four newborns did not survive.[3] The infant mortality rate in Hawaii in 1920 was 226 per 1000 births, more than twice the average of 95.7 per 1000 for all ethnic groups on the mainland.

Complex interrelationships involved demographic, social, and ethnic changes, as well as biological and economic factors. Due to immigration, the population in Hawaii increased rapidly, especially as "picture brides" arrived from Japan. The number of persons of all ages living in Hawaii more than doubled during the first third of the century, from approximately 150,000 at the time of U.S. annexation in 1898 to more than 360,000 by 1930—a rate of growth more than two times that of the mainland United States. Kauai reflected this remarkable change: The island's population grew from 20,562 in 1900 to 35,806 by 1930, mostly affected by the migration of workers from Japan and the Philippines.

The central fact of Hawaii's demographic changes, however, was the shift from a disproportionate number of males to a balanced gender population. There had been large numbers of unmarried male adults at the beginning of the twentieth century in Hawaii, but the number of females soon began to increase. Among Japanese-Americans, who constituted the largest percentage of Hawaii's population in 1900, the female population grew by as much as five times between 1900 and 1930, while the male population increased by 160 percent. It was estimated that almost half of these women were "picture brides."[4]

The growing percentage of married women in all ethnic groups, particularly those at childbearing ages, resulted in a full-fledged baby boom for Territorial Hawaii. The annual birthrate in the Islands rose from 25 births per 1000 in the 1910 population to a peak in 1920 of 42 births per 1000. This trend in marriages and births among the Japanese and Filipinos meant that new families would require better living spaces, as well as dependable home birthing and infant care help.

During and after the baby boom, a downward trend in the number of deaths on Kauai of infants under one year old was the consequence of several steps that helped women carry, bear, and raise healthier young children.

The education of new mothers took center stage, and understanding cleanliness, nutrition, and the prevention of infectious disease was important. The approach was partially the result of networking with other immigrant women, including newly arrived, trained midwives from Japan, Korea, and the Philippines. On Kauai, new mothers were also reached by the Mokihana Club, plantation nurses, and Mabel Wilcox. At the same time, new Territorial Board of Health policies improved sanitary conditions, and reforms in industrial housing by Hawaii's sugar plantations were aimed at relieving overcrowding and improving social conditions for labor.

The growing availability of ethnic midwives in Hawaii, and the ability of young families to afford midwife services, also encouraged care for mothers. Betty Sora, R.N., who grew up on Lihue Plantation, remembered some of her mother-in-law's birthing experiences:

> When she was in a child-bearing age, she would be going into labor and my father-in-law totally oblivious, or not paying even attention, and then he would get ready, early in the morning, to go to work. And then she would have to beg him, plead with him, 'Please get the midwife, because the time is coming.' And then you hear of other people just working so hard in the fields, going into labor, going into a corner, just squatting and delivering and then going back to work right away, but I didn't really witness that.[5]

Babies were delivered at home in plantation camp housing in isolated rural districts by midwives, family members, relatives, informal helpers, or plantation medical personnel. The services of midwives and their cultural home delivery practices were well established by 1910.[6] Midwives were more than birth attendants: they usually spoke the language of the mother and helped as nurses, housekeepers, and teachers. Some Asian women were trained formally as midwives before arriving on Kauai. They could be compared with many European-trained, skilled midwives on the mainland. One of the busiest of these midwives was Mrs. Kazuo Kuboyama of Eleele, a graduate of the Chosen Sotoku-fu in Korea in 1913, a five-year course, including nursing and midwivery training. Kazuo Koboyama first practiced in Japan following graduation and then came to Hawaii in 1919 as a picture bride on Kauai. She regularly delivered 40 to 50 babies a year on the west side of the island. Other midwives, like Mrs. Koto Takasawa of Hanapepe and Mrs. Tsumoru Iwamoto of Kapaa, were graduates of midwivery schools but had smaller practices. Guadalupe Bisande of Kapaa had no professional training but began practicing in the Philippines in 1906.

Mabel was responsible for initiating a small, voluntary program of infant welfare in 1916, concurrent with her work with TB. Mabel actively worked through the Mokihana Club to recruit a visiting maternal and child health nurse for the Lihue area. On Oahu, voluntary child health care services had been provided by the Free Kindergarten and Children's Aid Association, Kapiolani Maternity Home, Kauikeolani Children's Hospital, and Palama Settlement, all of them concerned with infant mortality. Supervised by James A. Rath, a social worker who had been trained in Springfield and Boston, Palama Settlement employed a staff of four district nurses by 1909, reflecting the far-reaching influence of other settlement houses on the mainland. During the following years, the settlement house helped other nurses enter the public health field. One of these, Mabel Leilani Smyth, was supported by Rath to attend the Springfield Hospital Training School for Nurses when she was nineteen. She returned to Oahu in 1915 and joined the staff of Palama Settlement, one of the first Hawaiian women to be certified for nursing. Smyth was appointed Palama's head nurse three years later and by the 1920s worked closely with Mabel as supervising Territorial public health nurse.[7]

The other Honolulu voluntary organization that greatly shaped family services was the Associated Charities of Hawaii (later split into the Social Services Bureau, Honolulu Community Chest, and United Way). It provided programs of foster care, fresh milk, a free dispensary, and cooperation with service clubs on Oahu. Margaret Bergen from Indianapolis joined the organization in 1914, and became director. Bergen pressed for maternal and child welfare and brought to Hawaii's early public health nurses and social workers a crusading approach, along with the benefit of her extensive settlement house and social work experience. A friend of the famous reformer Jane Addams at Hull House in Chicago, Bergen was familiar with the work of other contemporary "maternalists," as they were called in the United States and England, and she believed that more women should play active roles outside the home and that female leadership was essential in social welfare.[8] As historian Richard Meckel wrote in *Save the Babies,* "[The] maternal education campaign pursued by infant welfare stations and visiting nurses was largely funded and conducted by a variety of private agencies and organizations."

Mabel, as chairman of the Mokihana Club's public health committee, came to know both Bergen and Rath and turned to them to spearhead a visiting nurse program for Kauai. Responding to the club's concerns about Kauai mothers and newborn, Bergen visited Lihue, addressed the Club's members and Mabel asked her to help train the new Mokihana nurse. At another Club meeting, Rath discussed the value of district nursing. He assisted by providing supplies for the new nurse, Fanny Kuhlig, R.N., who came from Kauikeolani Children's Hospital in Honolulu. Mabel wrote to Dora Isenberg, "I met Miss Kuhlig and had a long talk. I told her frankly I was afraid she would come down and get restless and leave us in the lurch." Fanny Kuhlig was reassuring, however, and agreed to try the position for six months. "Everyone spoke so highly of her and I like her appearance and ideas, so I decided to engage her."[9]

With pledges of donations and a benefit fair in Lihue, the club funded the position. Mabel called it "an experiment," but she hoped that if the Mokihana district nurse proved successful, the club would be able to find continuing financial support from the east Kauai plantations and develop cooperation with plantation doctors and nurses. From her experiences with Palama Settlement and Samuel Mahelona Hospital, Mabel was more and more convinced about the importance of maternal and child health nursing on Kauai. She expressed her thoughts this way as early as 1916:

> The public health nurse in the broadest sense embraces the tuberculosis nurse, the child welfare nurse, the school nurse, the social service worker; in fact she is the homemaker, caring for the race from their prenatal state until they have passed on to the next cycle of existence.[10]

As the one Territorial nurse on Kauai, Mabel could not reach all the island's mothers and newborns, and though the new Mokihana visiting nurse was helpful, Mabel was spread thin. In the Lihue district alone she had to serve 5,000 persons from all cultural, economic, and language backgrounds.[11]

As part of her job requirements, the Mokihana nurse did maternity work, gave instructions to women about diet and infant feeding, and conducted the first plantation health surveys on Kauai. Some of these reports have been preserved in the Mokihana Club records and provide documentation of inadequate plantation camp health conditions and details of nutritional problems. As Mabel noted, the reports brought out not only the number and kinds of cases treated, but the evident relation of poor housing to poor health.[12]

The position's first occupant, Fanny Kuhlig, moved on after six months, and the next Mokihana nurse, Sarah Cheek, R.N., observed that "Alapaka" Camp as a whole is neither the best nor the poorest of the camps of Lihue Plantation, it is however the best of the camps at Hanamaulu." In 1919 she wrote about overcrowded dwellings and social environment:

> Conditions in this camp are such to lower all standards of living and morals. Three examples will serve to illustrate the point. In number 36, in a small dark room in the middle of the house, live a widow and her two small children, girls aged four and two years, in each of the other five rooms in the house live from three to five men. In number 33, in two rooms, lives a family of ten, a man, his wife, six children, son-in-law and grandchild, of these then six are over fourteen years of age and of both sexes. In number 38, in two rooms, lives a family of twelve, parents and ten children, six of these are over thirteen years and of both sexes. Often child-rearing had to be faced single-handedly. As one social analyst concluded, the work 'was more difficult because women were in a foreign cultural situation with new demands on their own as well as their children's behavior.'[13]

The reports by the Mokihana nurse also offer perspectives on child-rearing practices by Lihue plantation mothers:

> The nurse was requested to put special efforts on Infant Welfare. This she did and undertook to weigh all newborn babies once a week for one month and then once a month for six months. Also all cases of mal-nutrition were weighed once a week, others once in two weeks according to the case. This work was very interesting but exceedingly strenuous. The nurse was met with apparent indifference by a great number of families who disliked the interference and considered it a great nuisance to have their babies weighed. When school opened for the fall term, it was decided that the nurse should do school work and the general weighing of babies was discontinued. Cases of evident mal-nutrition have been weighed until such cases were in a good condition. As far as possible all cases of newborn babies are visited and the mothers given advice about the care and feeding of babies. ... All the babies are watched and general advice given to the mothers. It is the general custom throughout the camps to give the babies "Eagle Brand" milk as a substitute for breast milk. The nurse does not consider this a good food for babies and has endeavored to have the mothers use cow's milk or Dryco. In many cases this has

been accomplished but it is a very difficult problem because cow's milk costs $6.20 per month and Dryco about as much. The people cannot afford this. However, the nurse has had some cases, which have been very satisfactory. The mothers have used cow's milk or Dryco and carried forth a well regulated three hour schedule, asking for the advice of the nurse when a change in the amount given was necessary. In many cases babies are weaned from the breast when it is not necessary. The nurse has tried to make the mothers realize the value of breast milk. This is especially true of the Portuguese who say it is too much trouble to nurse the baby. Other cases nurse their babies until three or four years of age. This is especially true of the Japanese. The nurse has tried to teach these mothers the value of a normal diet. It is rather hard to put this to them so that they will appreciate the value of the information because they like their own way best.[14]

Plantation housing reforms in the first part of the century were influenced by complex concerns. They were a product of "Social Progressivism," a term some historians have used to describe early twentieth-century measures in the United States that contributed to improvements in industrial working conditions. As Carroll Pursell has put it, "One major stream of American Progressivism was that searching for social justice and humane institution. Another was an effort to rationalize and manage society in the interests of stability and order." For the Islands, social forces to be reckoned with included immigrant working-class ethnic groups, the demographic transition to married laborers (and Hawaii's population surge as a result), Territorial Board of Health public health programs, reform activities of voluntary social welfare organizations, and the paternalistic policies of the sugar industry itself. Progressivism in Hawaii linked the operators of plantations, discontented laborers, plantation doctors and nurses, government sanitary engineers from the Board of Health, and upper- and middle-class people involved in voluntary welfare associations together in a common cause.

Before 1920, the Territorial Board of Health and the Palama Street Settlement in Honolulu advocated the betterment of workers' housing, and both played active roles by providing plantations with construction plans, building a model home, and drawing attention to health problems caused by the old, inadequate structures.

The single-family house best represented the physical expression of healthy housing in Hawaii. New dwellings would be built with greater room differentiation, more windows with larger openings to improve cross-ventilation, inset porches or covered lanais, and extended roof eaves, which permitted windows to be kept open in most kinds of weather. For the first time, poured concrete—a long-wearing, fireproof, and easily maintained material—was introduced in the floor construction of some kitchens and wash houses. Most of the new houses were set apart on larger lots, many were enclosed by hedges or fences with yards for gardening, and they were connected to camp waterlines, providing a more hygienic water supply for food preparation, drinking, washing up, bathing, and laundry.[15]

The interrelated interests of the Board of Health and social welfare professionals in reform housing had a direct influence on individual plantations. Between 1917 and 1920, for example, Grove Farm put up 120 houses west of Lihue in a single new camp for workers called Puhi Camp. George Wilcox, Charles Wilcox, their manager Edward H. W. Broadbent, and Mabel and Elsie, with their familiarity with the Board of Health and social welfare work, were responsible for building the new camp.[16]

In 1919, the Hawaiian Sugar Planters' Association (HSPA) would establish a Social Welfare Bureau, acting as a planning catalyst for individual plantations. The Bureau would provide operators with detailed surveys of living conditions on their plantations, conducted by an experienced social worker. It would follow up by preparing and distributing sets of standard blueprints and bills of construction materials, demonstrating the Association's role as a centralized organization.

Better-informed mothers, Board of Health sanitation measures, plantation housing reforms coupled with trained midwives, the Territorial tuberculosis nurse, and the voluntary, health education work of the Mokihana Club nurses, produced significant results. Kauai was part of a rapidly changing physical, biological, and social environment, and between 1912 and 1924 the infant mortality rate for all groups in Hawaii was reduced by half—from about 200 per 1000 infants a year to 100 per 1000. As Richard Meckel has said of similar prevention steps on the Mainland:

> [N]o other modern reduction of mortality—not that accomplished among older children and adults by the virtual eradication of tuberculosis, nor that effected by the diminution of venereal disease,—comes near comparing with the reduction of infant mortality.[17]

The first years of Mabel's long career as a nurse and in community affairs were intertwined with the health problems of Kauai and the responses of the Territory of Kauai, plantations, and voluntary women's associations like the Mokihana Club. In the years before 1920 the groups worked hand in hand. Mabel's career took a dramatic turn in 1917, however, when the United States declared war on Germany. As part of military mobilization, Mabel was sent to France by the Red Cross to treat suffering Belgian and French refugees. It was a demanding experience which directly drew upon her training on Kauai and prepared her for leadership in the new field of maternal and child health and public nursing after the war.

Chapter Seven

WAR NURSE

Mabel was the general manager at Mahelona Hospital for only a few months before the First World War interrupted her work at the new sanatorium and on the Mokihana Club's visiting nurse project. "I'd always been a Red Cross nurse," Mabel recalled many years after the war. She had written to the Chairman of the National Committee on Red Cross Nursing Service, Jane Delano, about enrollment of nurses from Hawaii even before the United States entered the war. She looked forward to an assignment in the Johns Hopkins Military Base Hospital Red Cross nursing unit with a sense of patriotism. The Chief Nurse at Johns Hopkins Hospital, Bessie Baker, R.N., wrote to Mabel on Kauai that should there be war, "it is a great comfort to know that you are ready and willing to go." [1]

Mabel said later, "They sent a cable in 1917 when the war began for the United States, but the cable was sent to the Philippines by mistake." When the Red Cross order came for the Hopkins unit to mobilize, other cablegrams to Mabel were sent.

"A message came that second time," Mabel recalled:

I was swimming in Hanalei. They called here, my father got the message and sent it through to the Deverills at Hanalei and they in turn called me out of swimming. The telegram was asking me to join the Johns Hopkins unit. I resigned my job here, hurriedly getting my relief.

Having not gotten a response from the first telegram to the Philippines, Baker decided that Mabel should go to the East Coast to wait for another detachment of nurses and wrote to say how disappointed she was that Mabel would not be able to be part of the unit. Mabel sailed for the mainland in August:

> I went to Hopkins, found that the unit had already gone and that my place had been filled.

> I went to the Washington head of Red Cross who was a Hopkins woman. The Army wanted to send me down South, [I] would never have gotten overseas. [The] Washington head of Red Cross nurses said there was no opening then but would keep me in mind. I said I'd go to Columbia to study until called, to take courses in advance nursing and public health. I was there six weeks when I was asked if I would take a group of nurses' aides to Europe.[2]

At Teachers College, Columbia University, the Department of Nursing and Health was directed by the renowned nurse, M. Adelaide Nutting. With its emphasis on hospital administration and public health, the new program was innovating post graduate training. During Mabel's brief stay in New York, she attended classes and lived in a small hotel room with her cousin Helen Lyman and with Ethel Damon, who had come from Honolulu to volunteer for Red Cross duty. Mabel remained resolved to serve overseas, however. Writing to her mother from New York in November, she described meeting with Clara Noyes, the Director of the Red Cross Bureau of Nursing, who made amends for the Red Cross mix-up.

> Tuesday I went to Baltimore and on Wednesday to Washington to see Miss Noyes of the Nursing Service who had sent for me. She asked me first if I would come into the office. It would have been tremendously interesting and right in touch with everything, but I was afraid I'd never get out, so I said I'd rather "go over." That I felt I'd missed going with the Unit because Miss Baker thought Hawaii was in the P.I. & probably sent the cable there first. She was very much amused at Miss Baker … she wanted to let me go to France because of it. So I should be going soon.[3]

Mabel was part of an American mobilization that processed personnel, food, supplies and ships to help the war-weary Allies. As many as 20,000 Red Cross nurses—about a tenth of America's nurses—went overseas for military and civilian duty during the First World War. They were part of the two million Americans transported to France in 1917 to 1918 and they served at the front (like the Hopkins unit), or helped battered, dispirited, and sick French and Belgian civilians in dispensaries opened in French cities like Le Havre where Mabel was assigned. Red Cross nurses contributed to emergency support for mothers and children whose lives were impacted by the

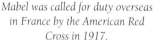

Mabel was called for duty overseas in France by the American Red Cross in 1917.

calamity, and they played a key role in caring for victims who had been displaced by battle.[4]

In October 1917 Washington wired Mabel in New York to take 13 Red Cross nurses' aides to France. There were delays, but in December they sailed to Bordeaux aboard the French passenger ship *S.S. Espagnol*. Mabel was given directions to hand over the aides to Red Cross headquarters in Paris where she would receive her own orders. As their chaperone, she found the semi-trained volunteer aides "very nice girls, most of them seem to have sense." "They promise quite well even if they are society ladies," she confided in a letter to Daisy in Lihue with characteristic candor and dry wit (as well as a hint of the class struggles she herself would face in France). After overhearing one of her aides at the New York steamship office order a clerk not to give her any dirty money in change, "I said I thot she would find a good many worse things than dirty money in France."

"Our trip was uneventful as far as submarines were concerned," she commented. During the ocean crossing she wrote, "Canteen workers, Surgical Dressings, Y.M.C.A., both men and women, the latter Secretaries, and a large Commission to Italy. ... One can't move without meeting them." Former classmates in Baltimore had given her a letter of introduction to Edwards Park, M.D., a Johns Hopkins Hospital pediatrician who was also on board. Park had been in charge of the Hopkins hospital dispensary with research interests in malnutrition. After they met, Park recognized Mabel's experience. "We used to walk the decks," she said.[5]

On the last day of the crossing, Mabel later wrote that the ship "had received an S.O.S. wireless message from about fifty miles away. ... I had seen the hull of a torpedoed boat and much wreckage floating by." She added, "I think we were all more relieved than any of us cared to admit to land safely at Bordeaux."

The First World War gave American nurses many new responsibilities. The two Red Cross nurses in charge of placing all arriving personnel in Paris were the Chief Nurse of the American Red Cross Commission for France, Martha Russell, R.N., and Elizabeth Ashe, R.N., Chief Nurse of the Children's Bureau. They met Mabel and her charges at Red Cross headquarters in Place de la Concorde, and, after the initial interviews were over, Mabel noted, "as soon as we could we went to Miss Ashe's office. She is head of the Children's Bureau, and is a wonder." Ashe had been Director of the Telegraph Hill Neighborhood Association in San Francisco before coming to France, and Mabel and she talked about tuberculosis and infant welfare nursing on Kauai. Ashe told Mabel she wanted her to work in her bureau. "I was certainly delighted for the Public Health work among the women and children is a wonderful piece of work." Ashe was "very much interested in my work out there." She explained the gravity of wartime conditions in France to Mabel, including depopulation. The decline in France's birthrate was the opposite of the baby boom in Hawaii. This trend in France was a potential national catastrophe; two French adults were dying for every child born during the war.

Ashe introduced Mabel to the Associate Chief of the Red Cross Children's Bureau, J.H. Mason Knox, M.D., Mabel first met Knox at Johns Hopkins and she recalled, "I worked in 1912 at his baby hospital near Baltimore. ... He of course didn't remember me." Knox, a pioneer specialist in nutritional preventive infant care, was also a member of the Hopkins pediatrics faculty. He was a medical superintendent and director of the Mt. Wilson Hospital in Baltimore for infants and children and one of the founders of the philanthropic Baltimore Babies Milk Association. Both Knox and his Hopkins colleague Park were socially conscious clinicians and advocates of maternal and child health care centers, whose creation had already produced success in American cities like Baltimore, New York, Boston, and Buffalo.

The Red Cross Children's Bureau began with relief work for refugee children but its long-term purpose was to help the French establish a national child welfare program. They were committed, as were all public health reformers, to planning public health activities "along scientific lines by a scientifically trained elite, and not left either to the good intentions of amateurs or to changing political purposes of special interests."[6]

Beyond meetings with this talented circle in the bustling headquarters, Mabel visited Paris hospitals, women's charitable dispensaries, and day nurseries. She also began taking daily lessons in conversational French. "My efforts at French are remarkable—the other day I stopped somewhere for tea, and thot I'd order tea and some of those wonderful little cakes France is famous for. Instead of the cakes appeared war bread and cheese," she reported disappointedly. She wrote in her diary on December 23, 1917:

> Breakfast in bed—a call from Mlle. Cogelin who is to talk French an hour every day with me. Miss Ashe dined at our table & afterwards came to my rooms where we had Washington coffee & a conference on nursing affairs & conditions most interesting & illuminating. In the evening to the Opera to hear Samson & Delila—wonderful.[7]

Mabel was not the only nurse from Hawaii to go overseas. Several Honolulu nurses had volunteered before America entered the war and joined the British Nursing Service. Among others from the Islands sent to France as nurses, physicians, and nurses' aides were Stella S. Mathews R.N., James R. Judd, M.D., and his wife Louise M. Judd. Mathews later became the superintendent of Hilo Memorial Hospital and head nurse at Palama Settlement. In France, she was put in charge of nurses at a Red Cross base hospital in 1918, and after the war she went to Poland and Greece to supervise the expansion of Red Cross health centers in Europe. Judd, who earlier had helped Mabel with her admission to Johns Hopkins, volunteered in 1915 with his wife for the American Ambulance Field Service.

Judd served as a surgeon at two hospitals in France, and Mrs. Judd became a Red Cross nurses' aide.[8] Mabel unsuccessfully tried to see the Judds in Paris when she took her aides to tour the American Ambulance Hospital at Neuilly. She commented on a Red Cross Director of Aides who met her at the American Hospital:

> Mrs. Monroe, a wealthy banker's wife, who seems to be sort of Lady Bountiful of the place and to have charge of the Aides there took us thru ... . But with such a party and without a nurse what we saw was very superficial ... I asked twice to see the Honolulu

ward, said I came from H. and knew Dr. Judd ... but Lady Bountiful thought we were only insignificant Nurses and Aides! [9]

Such occasions would be common throughout her experience in France.

Mabel was in Paris for Christmas of 1917, and she gave her Red Cross aides a party before they were sent off to posts throughout France. "We see lots of soldiers in uniform, and wounded soldiers on the streets and so much mourning," she wrote. During the holidays, the Englishwoman who ran the small Hotel d'Jena, near the Eiffel Tower where she was staying, also gave a party for 50 soldiers from Australia and New Zealand. They were "all fine, splendid fellows." The merriment was interrupted by an air-raid alert, and "at 10:30 quite a number of the boys had to leave for the front and they were a sorry bunch. The others stayed until twelve, playing games and dancing and had a fine time, and so did we." When she moved to another hotel used by the Y.W.C.A. she wrote, "There are no end of wahines here, and the occasional man who strays in is indeed brave. I can stand it while the cold weather lasts, as it is very comfortable, but if I were in Paris, I'd want to be away from the Americans and hear French and see an occasional man!"[10]

Mabel believed that she might be sent north to Amiens to help set up a children's dispensary close to French and British lines. She was given time to "get out into the work being done in Paris, in the way of settlements and dispensaries—in this way I can size up things and get ready for Amiens." Waiting for orders on December 30, however, she wrote of the possibility that she might be retained at Paris headquarters, but she also speculated that Park had persuaded Ashe that she was needed in Le Havre to become his head nurse. She reflected in her diary, "If I didn't keep busy it would be so easy to be homesick, but I imagine Havre will be worse than this. C'est la guerre!"

Kauai seemed a million miles away, and wartime separation started to catch up with her. She received notes, letters, packages, and newspapers from Hawaii but, as her diary shows, Mabel missed her family and the intimacy of her close-knit community. She reported on January 6, 1918:

> Still in Paris and still uncertain as to my final destination. Every time I report at Headquarters I am told of something different, alternating with Dr. Park's request of me . His detail is to start work at Le Havre among the Belgians chiefly, altho we will do any work that comes to hand. He tells me that it promises to be a big thing,

the Belgian government gives some help, and we would have more or less of a free hand away from red tape, to start dispensaries, hospitals, visiting work, and in fact anything we may find of use. … I am anxious to go with Dr. Park, altho I am afraid it is too big a proposition for me to handle, and I hope that when he is out of sight I won't be thrust elsewhere. He simply wants me because I'm a Hopkins nurse. … He seems like a very nice fellow and I think I'll be lucky to be placed with him. Meanwhile I'm glad to be in Paris, comfort-loving creature that I am, I'm enjoying hot baths and steam heat as long as possible. … Wish I could really write & describe conditions over here, but everything is so strange & confused & tremendous that it is difficult to even think.[11]

Chapter Eight

"A PERFECT MEDICAL UNIT"

Mabel finally received Red Cross orders assigning her as a head nurse to Le Havre. Her experience building the Samuel Mahelona Memorial Hospital was fresh in her mind as she wrote from Paris, "[H]ave gone over lists of equipment, etc. I'd give a million for my lists and catalogues that I had for the S.M.M. Hospital." A few days before she left Paris she said, "Miss Ashe, my chief said yesterday she wished she could get her hands on me for she needed 25 nurses on the spot! I only grinned and hoped to goodness she wouldn't change her mind about letting Dr. Park have me."[1]

The French possessed no group of public health nurses comparable to that which existed in the United States and Britain. The Red Cross organized clinical welfare dispensaries in 18 towns throughout France, not including Paris, during the war. The Belgian government and the American Red Cross Children's Bureau agreed to establish one of its model health centers for mothers and children in impoverished districts of Le Havre. The peacetime population of most French cities increased greatly during four traumatic years of war with Germany.[2] Le Havre became congested with more than 20,000 displaced Belgian civilian evacuees, including government officials; the coastal city was also a major harbor for newly arrived Allied military forces. The size of Le Havre had increased from 150,000 persons to about 220,000 French, Belgian, and other Allies. Faced with problems of food rationing and inflation, Mabel observed, "This surplus population had been forced to find lodgings in a city already filled to its normal capacity, for not a single new building had been erected anywhere." Living conditions were miserable, and Mabel reported:

The crowding in the poorer parts of the city was so extreme that

whole families lived in single rooms. The rents that refugees and
other newcomers were obliged to pay were more than three times
their pre-war value. The prices of food, coal (which was rationed),
clothes and household supplies had at least tripled.[3]

Mabel noted, "Most French and Belgian Drs. had been mobilized.
As a result, suffering among the people caused by unhygienic
conditions, scarcity of food, vermin and neglect was very common."
The French agencies and local social services were all understaffed,
and the few physicians who remained in Le Havre "were for the most
part occupied with clientele able to pay."[4] In January 1918 she wrote
to her family, "I could tell you endlessly of the stories of these children
but they are mostly too heart-rending." She wanted to get to work
quickly and concentrate on what needed to be done.[5]

Mabel's firsthand descriptions of wartime civilian conditions in
her diary, letters home, and later notes contained insights into the
organization of one of the Red Cross health centers and her day-to-day
experiences as its head nurse. She and the others on the Red Cross
Children's Bureau's small staff in Le Havre saw the disruptive results
of the war everywhere they went, including physiological problems
of malnutrition and the epidemics of childhood diseases that swept
through the civilian refugee population. They quickly learned to
understand that devastating losses of life in battle, combined with
France's low birth rate and growing fear of depopulation, meant
that the country's future chances of recovering from war casualties
depended heavily on the care of the young. Mabel later said:

> The first work was done with the refugees, the poor people who
> were driven in great crowds from their homes by the advance
> of the German army. I know you have all seen pictures of that
> procession of men, women and children, donkey carts, goat carts,
> wheelbarrows, cows, horses, dogs, sadly fleeing from their homes
> which were no longer homes.

The French government turned over an old building, Salle
Franklin, at the center of the overcrowded central part of Le Havre for
the care of both Belgian and French families. The former workingmen's
club, named for Benjamin Franklin, had been converted into a military
hospital earlier in the war. As Mabel put it,

> The Salle is quite a large, rambling place, and has many possibilities
> as well as more impossibilities. It is surely French in being dirty
> with dirt of ages, and in being unsanitary as to plumbing ... How
> I wish I could have the S.M.M. Hosp.!

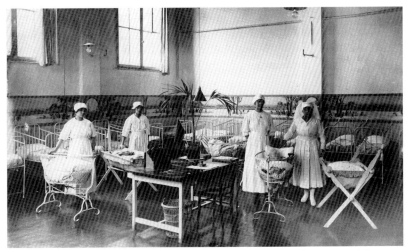

Staffed by Belgian "Lady Patrons", French and American nurses and assistants, Salle Franklin was a workingman's club in Le Havre converted by the Red Cross Children's Bureau for care of Belgian and French refugee infants and mothers.

Salle Franklin had been vacant for several months, and Mabel reported that French "lady patrons" responsible for the hospital "were very angry over the fact that a Reserve *Military* Hospital was to be turned over for Civilian work & for Belgians!" Moreover the "lady patrons" maintained existing French class distinctions. Mabel complained about them trying to get their own way: "might as well stop an ocean wave as a hysterical, chittering, unreasonable French woman." As Alisa Klauss writes in *Every Child a Lion*, a comparative history of the origins of maternal and infant welfare in France and the United States, French female patronesses were a voluntary women's association and "a critical force in the transition from private charity to public welfare." Klauss explains, "Unlike American visiting nurses, who claimed authority based on their training, the French were deemed qualified to supervise and instruct other women by virtue of their social position." As a territorial nurse in Hawaii, Mabel had been treated as a professional but she saw fundamental differences between her experiences with the "lady patrons" in France and women like Dora Rice Isenberg and the Mokihana Club members.[6]

There were only a few American staff in Le Havre, and Mabel was the only American graduate nurse on staff. The small group at Salle Franklin depended greatly on one another. She boarded at the same *pension* with Edwards Park and Ernest Bicknell and his family. Park's English born wife had left Baltimore for England to stay with her parents while he was in France.

Bicknell was a former national director of the American Red Cross and the director general of the American Red Cross Civilian Relief in France and Italy and commissioner for Belgium. He had brought his wife and daughter to live at Le Havre with him.

The most desperate single condition in Le Havre was housing the swollen population. Mrs. Bicknell said "to the overcrowded, unsanitary, and dark lodgings which the refugees were forced to occupy at the cost, exorbitant to them, of fifty francs a room a month, could be laid many of the evils of disease and family disintegration." As the staff began its work with mothers and children, Park found it fortuitous for the health center plans that Mabel had brought a letter of introduction to Bicknell from Margaret Bergen, in Honolulu. Bergen was one of Bicknell's social service administrative peers, both sharing a background in welfare reform.[7] "Ernest Bicknell wanted me at Le Havre right away to get organized to care for refugee children from Belgium," Mabel said.

Le Havre was 200 miles from the front in early 1918. Mabel visited the nearby French and British military hospitals in Normandy and observed the British Army base, several Belgian munitions plants, and the harbor convoys coming and going, bringing supplies and other preparations for defense against an expected German offensive. By February Mabel and Park were working on plans for the dispensary, deciding on the arrangement and effective use of waiting rooms, consultation and examination chambers, medical and social services offices, a bacteriological laboratory, and a pharmacy in the old hall. They identified staffing needs for their operational plans: there would be French and Belgian nurses, and Park requested a second pediatrician and a nurses' aide. He asked the Red Cross for one of his Johns Hopkins Medical School pediatric graduates, Alma Rotholz, M.D., and she soon was on her way from Baltimore. One of Park's goals was to make Salle Franklin a center of efficient, professionally run public health service.[8]

Mabel heard from Ethel Damon in New York and she wrote home: "In Ethel's letter, she said she might come over in canteen work. I had asked for her as secretary-interpreter for our work here ... she may not want to change from Canteen to Children but we certainly need her and can make use of her. ... When I told Dr. Park about her and how fluent she was in French, he put in for her."[9] Ethel was put in charge of record keeping, including medical appointments. She maintained the forms for patient histories, consultations and prescriptions at Salle Franklin and wrote home to her sister in Honolulu about Paris and Le Havre:

I reached Le Havre from Paris on March 25th having experienced the first gloomy day there of the attack by Big Bertha, the long range gun. Since then I have been in charge of all the records, registrations, correspondence and purchasing of the rapidly growing office. And since no stenographer could be had until September, my little Corona certainly has done good service. Technically I am a nurse's aid, but was recently elevated, at the end of my six months contract, to the position of secretary and business manager to Dr. Park. My occupations continue to be the same, everything from buying toothpicks and settling servants' quarrels to paying salaries and initiating reports of work to the Queen of Belgium.

Ethel had waited in Paris for Mabel who was coming to the city with Dr. Park. Before Mabel and Dr. Park arrived, however, there was an air raid:

Almost immediately the whole city went pitch black. I preferred going on to the station but decided that I might miss M. in the dark even if she got as far as the city … After waiting for a while on the ground floor I groped my way into the cellar where half of the hotel guests were merrily assembled in various stages of day and night dress. I gave M. up entirely and was just thinking about the prospects of a night's sleep in an armchair, when someone called to me that my friends from Honolulu had arrived. And sure enough, there she was, with tall Dr. Park, both grinning in the light of a single electric flash.[10]

Carpenters, plumbers, painters, and other workmen were arriving to repair Salle Franklin. Bicknell's assistant in Le Havre and Deputy Commissioner of the American Red Cross Commission to Belgium was John van Schaick. He was responsible for coordinating the repairs of the Salle with *Belgique Libre*, the members of the Belgian civil government in Le Havre. Mabel was put off by her first meeting with Mrs. van Schaick, who was also staying in Le Havre with her husband. "Had a note from Mr. Van Schiack [sic] asking me to dine with them at 7:30. Mrs. Van S. in for a minute when I arrived (Thinks I'm a nurse not a lady)." It would be the start of Mabel's edgy relationship with both van Schaicks.

At the front, Germany moved reinforcements, and its troops made ready for another attack against the Allied lines.

The offensive is still holding off. I suppose every day counts for us & our preparations. You hear a good many people say that an offensive would be the best possible thing for us, as we are so absolutely ready that it would mean terrible loses for the Germans not only in men but in morale, & that it would hurt the [German] military party terribly.[11]

In March 1918, the Germans took the offensive, breaking through British and French lines and launching a follow-up blow in Flanders in April. Allied forces, including American troops, helped break the German advance at Chateau-Thierry and Belleau Wood, and the Western front again was stabilized by May. By then, however, another thousand homeless, dazed French refugees from the German offensive arrived in Le Havre needing care.

As a result of the German offensive the renovation of Salle Franklin took longer than had been expected. In March Mabel observed, "We haven't progressed on our hospital, in fact at present it isn't at all certain whether we will stay in Havre." Although van Schaick's later official account of Red Cross work did not mention it, she and Park could not conceal their resentment and agitation when, without their prior knowledge, van Schaick informed them both that Belgian government ministers had appointed their own committee of politically chosen Belgian Lady Patrons to take administrative charge of most of the departments at Salle Franklin. "We were to sit by & be figureheads or something, and gradually were to be pushed out," she wrote. She criticized van Schaick in her diary, "Then the matter of our separation from Paris Bureau brot up. Dr. V.S. very nasty and disagreeable ... I think we had better leave with the feeling that Dr. V.S. evidently has against us."[12]

It made matters worse when Mrs. van Schaick became sick with a cold, Mabel was "requested or ordered I don't know which," to take care of her. She wrote home to her mother, "So I've had the pleasure for two weeks of attending her, much to my rage. She wouldn't ask the maid to do anything but waited for her to offer – so I've been doing all the maid's cleaning etc. I finally wrote a sarcastic letter to Paris & asked for a withdrawal from Havre."[13]

As anger and disappointment increased, Knox finally came out from Paris headquarters to meet with the representatives of the Belgian government and with Bicknell, van Schaick, Park, and Wilcox. Mabel later commented:

We have been trying to get Dr. Knox up here for weeks, but he seemed to think we could get along somehow, however when he got here he found the arrangements made by the Belgian Gov't. &

consented to by Mr. v. Schaick, such that we could absolutely do no work.

Dr. Knox got a good taste of this & he was furious, pitched into the Belgian Gov't. & Mr. V. S. & gave them 24 hours in which to make up their minds as to our work here. Dr. Knox and Dr. Park ordered me back to Paris to find new equipment and got me off Mrs. Van Schaick's case.[14]

To proceed with medical relief work, the Red Cross officials agreed to separate the departments at Salle Franklin. The Belgians, it was decided, would direct obstetrics, and Park, Wilcox, and staff would conduct the children's dispensary and operate the new children's hospital. "We have started some of our work with the Belgians altho our Dispensary won't be ready for some time," Mabel wrote in April. The French government also requested that the facility add care for French refugees in Le Havre. Mabel's comment was, "We have waited all along to combine work for both, but the two nationalities are not very friendly."[15]

Mabel was affected by conditions she could not control. Tensions created by war and bias in the structure of hierarchies around her continued to make her impatient, and she resented the Schaicks' manipulative personalities. Mabel described an audience she and Park had with a Belgian *grande dame* upon whom the van Schaicks lavished much attention and flattery. The Belgian countess informed them that each Belgian woman at Salle Franklin had hired her own nurses and servants. "Each one expected to be Lady of all creation in the Salle Franklin," Mabel concluded. The countess had turned to Mabel Wilcox during this meeting and asked condescendingly what she was doing there. "As I came to be in charge of the Salle Franklin & that I was to engage nurses etc., I was rather stumped for a tactful reply," Mabel wrote. She managed to answer that she was in Le Havre for "children's work."[16] Her final word on this came when she later wrote:

> There promises to be endless work if we could only get away from the fuss & fuddle of Belgian permissions & grants etc. They seem to think everything has to be done by Ladies Committees & Countesses etc & as Dr. Park says 'they at present are running around & making perfect asses of themselves' while we wait on the side lines until their burst of enthusiasm is over. Patience is the biggest virtue one needs over here. But I'll guarantee that soon we will be so busy we can't see.[17]

From the time the Salle Franklin dispensary opened its doors in April 1918, the new American Red Cross child health program in Le Havre grew by leaps and bounds, and the staff were incessantly active. In only five months, more than 5,000 sick babies and children were treated at the dispensary, hospital branch clinics in the city, and during house visits. While Mabel continued to write home, the next five months she was too busy to make her daily diary entries. She noted the use of available resources in one letter home:

> "It is certainly a crude disp. & none of our supplies have come, but despite this we are doing a rushing business—and the old saying that Johns Hopkins people are strong on 'kind words and cold water' is coming true even over here."[18]

Park diagnosed symptoms of disease and treated children without much more than scales, tongue depressors, and a few medicines. Some of the Belgian Red Cross openly doubted if the staff could reach the refugee families. Mabel wrote, "The Countesses said that the Belgians would feel we were intruding into private houses & would feel injured if we Americans made visits into the homes. With our Belgian nurse we go right ahead & everywhere so far have been most gladly received." Work was extended beyond the refugees, and Mabel noted, "We have certainly found some terribly pathetic cases in just these few days." They treated cases of eczema, scabies, worms, running ears, diarrhea, and tuberculosis, and the staff vaccinated more than 1,000 school children during a threatened smallpox epidemic. Mabel described one case of women's hardships during the war:

> One day a mother with two girls, one thirteen, the other seven, came in. Hardly had they seated themselves to await their turn to see the Dr. when the older girl turned deathly white and nearly fainted,—after a glass of water she felt better but soon began vomiting. Upon examination and questioning we found this story—the family were refugees from Lille, a city in the northern part of France.. They, with the father who had tuberculosis had fled to Paris, where the father soon died, they had remained in Paris until air raids had frightened them on to Le Havre. The mother had been ill and had not been able to work, their money was almost gone, food was scarce and for ten days the mother and older girl had only once a day a cup of black coffee and one piece of black war bread,—they had given more to the little girl so that she was not suffering,—but Mother and Suzanne were in bad condition.[19]

WWI Poster collected by Mabel Wilcox "En Belgique les Belges ont faim. Tombola artistique" (In Belgium the Belgians are hungry. Artistic raffle) Color Lithograph by artist Théophile Alexandre Steinien Paris: Lapina, [1915] Illustration: A group of hungry Belgians holding food pails.

Because it combined both clinical and social medicine, Park referred to Salle Franklin as a model institution. Park, like the public health experts who would come after him, believed that the reduction in mortality could be explained primarily in terms of improvements in the environment, greater food supplies, and preventive medicine. Park knew that, in many instances, food was more important than medicine.

"Besides dispensing drugs & prescriptions we will give out food tickets and food prescriptions," Mabel noted. Park explained how the food was dispensed:

It became apparent that many of our patients needed food more than anything else, and that some arrangement must be made by which it could be supplied them. Accordingly, we made this matter the subject of a special report to Colonel Bicknell … and submitted the proposal that the American Red Cross place at our disposal certain food supplies then in its warehouses in Le Havre. Further, we suggested an arrangement with several stores of Le Havre by which orders for special foods issued by us and presented at the stores by our patients would be honored. Colonel Bicknell immediately acquiesced. He placed in our storeroom considerable quantities of wheat flour, sweetened and unsweetened condensed milk, and cocoa, while two of our nurses effected an arrangement with the stores in question, which put at our command fresh milk, eggs, rice, rice flour, potatoes, fresh vegetables and meat.[20]

Mabel reinforced Park's views that most public health issues in Le Havre were questions of the population congestion in the city, poor housing conditions, and a low standard of living. She worked with a committee of French civilians to investigate conditions and organize the issuance of food to patients. "The regulation of diet has been a prominent feature of the treatment from the very beginning," the committee reported, adding that "[c]areful investigation of social conditions in every case thus treated became a necessity." Addressing the profound concerns over France's population problems, they concluded that, "It is felt that a definite and scientific beginning has been made against infant mortality!"

Park taught the practical skills needed to operate Salle Franklin as a maternal and child health center, and little was left to chance. Park developed a series of questions for patients that nurses' aides were required to memorize "until its questions had become more or less second nature." Similarly, he adapted the record charts he used in children's service at Johns Hopkins Hospital Dispensary and emphasized the importance of keeping continuous and complete clinical and social notes of their cases. Park also inaugurated a patient appointment system at Salle Franklin. He wrote in 1919:

[T]he dispensary system generally in use, according to which the patients are obliged to assemble before 9 a.m. or 2 p.m. and then to wait often the whole morning or afternoon, implies that the time of the dispensary patient is of so little value that it may be almost disregarded. The truth is that the modern dispensary is conducted, primarily, with a view to the convenience of the dispensary physician, on the principle that it is better for forty patients seated on the benches to lose sixty hours' time, than for the doctors to be subjected to the possibility of losing one-half hour's time. As everyone who has worked in children's dispensaries knows, many a parent who finds himself obliged to sacrifice his day's wage, or, if he works at night, his day's sleep, will not bring his child to the dispensary.[21]

The Americans at Salle Franklin continued to steadily expand their services during the summer of 1918. Lady patrons notwithstanding, the

Red Cross Children's Bureau enlarged its staff to meet the needs of child patients at the dispensary, as well as in the newly constructed, barrack-style hospital built on the grounds, and in follow-up visits with families. By August, the staff was working intensively in the Quartier St. Francois: every mother of a newborn was visited and encouraged to bring her baby to the clinic for medical advice and treatment. The doctors also attended two weekly *Gouttes de Lait*, French milk feeding stations for babies, and they visited young patients at a tuberculosis dispensary. Ruth Washburn, a social service special worker, and pediatricians Molly Crawford, M.D., and Ruth Guy Dieuaide, M.D., were added to Park's Le Havre staff along with new nurses and aides. One of Park's colleagues at Hopkins later said: "Dr. Park's ambition was to establish a perfect medical unit for the care of young children in Le Havre."[22]

From all accounts the staff achieved their goals. Along with other duties, Park gave Mabel responsibility for planning the new children's hospital next to Salle Franklin, a job which allowed her, once again, to use her talents in architecture. She wrote her mother, "You will be interested to know that once more I'm deep in hospital plans. … So I'm back at my favorite past-time of drawing plans. Who would have thot that I'd be planning & equipping a hospital in France!" She also noted "Our barrack hospital is nearly finished—it is a portable affair and comes all in sections & is screwed or bolted all together—they are supposed to be able to use them again after the war." She designed the interior with partitions so that each child would have a small

A portable, barrack-style children's hospital was built on the grounds of Salle Franklin in 1918 by the Red Cross. Mabel Wilcox was Head Nurse of the hospital and public health dispensary, directed by John Hopkins pediatrician Edwards Park, M.D.

room, and there also was a sunroom for convalescents. "I think it will be very nice when it is finished—of course neither a Johns Hopkins or a Samuel Mahelona but quite adequate for a War Hospital, quite luxurious in fact with gas to cook by and electric lights to see by." She also described one of her problems: "We are told we can't have any more nurses—and of course nurses are needed desperately in military hospitals & of course they have much the greater need. I'm getting hold of aides and am going to train them for anything."[23]

The Red Cross met the need of training French nurses for child welfare work at its health centers, and Mabel also planned a two-month school in theory and practice for *visiteurs d'hygiene* that included lectures, conferences, and field work.

The effectiveness of Salle Franklin can be measured both qualitatively and quantitatively. Visiting nurses and aides, for example, received emotional support from many French families in Le Havre who accepted their care and were appreciative of the Red Cross's child welfare work. The popularity of the dispensary and clinics also had an amusing side. As Mabel wrote,

> Our work here grows daily and at present the A.R.C. Drs. & Disp. are all the fashion—with the result that we get quite a number of cases that are absolutely normal, so we have almost a detective agency at the door to enquire into the real needs.[24]

It was difficult to be granted leave by Paris Red Cross headquarters, so Park took matters into his own hands by the end of July. He sent Mabel and Ethel for a long weekend to a nearby coastal town, their first break in three months. They were joined by Ruth Rotholz and thoroughly enjoyed a brief vacation and one another's companionship. "I expected to do a lot of letter writing but didn't write one letter even," Mabel admitted. She added, "we slept late every morning then either went on the beach or the cliffs for the rest of the day ... I always fell asleep again promptly—but even so managed to acquire a wonderful coat of tan and to shake a miserable cold I had."[25] On the pretext of "seeing a sick uncle, " Park also was able to get away on leave from Le Havre to meet his wife in England. Mabel wrote good-naturedly that the staff at Salle Franklin had a "wonderful rest" during his absence:

> He is certainly fine but rather hard to work with—not because he is disagreeable, but because he is so absentminded—if he gets a worm under the microscope he forgets that there are such things as patients and we have the delightful job of pacifying irate patients sometimes for hours.[26]

Beachside R&R for Mabel Wilcox (center) and Ethel Damon (right) near Le Havre.

Medical historians have observed that "the Hopkins department of pediatrics had an unusually large number of female house officers, in part because department head Edwards A. Park was known to be sympathetic to the idea of women doctors." Throughout his career in medicine, in contrast to many of his colleagues, he advocated having women in responsible health care positions. Park's attitude towards his three pediatric colleagues and his backing of Mabel and her nursing staff at Salle Franklin, contributed to a respectful, mutually supportive work environment.[27] Park and Rotholz reinforced Mabel's professional education. She found it a "rare chance" to be working with Park, and she also appreciated Rotholz's skills. "It certainly is fine getting back to work with real Drs. & getting in touch with medical things again. My T.B. work certainly made me rusty."

As American military forces in France continued to increase, the Allies began their sustained offensive in August 1918. The British army broke the German front, and the war tide began to turn. In September, during the offensive, Mabel was sent into Belgium to inspect maternal and child health conditions directly behind advancing lines in West Flanders; she stayed in Belgium for a month and witnessed part of the final campaign that led to the Armistice.

In anticipation of the Allied offensive, Park was assigned additional responsibilities as Red Cross Medical Director for unoccupied Belgium and van Schaick urged the extension of the Red Cross children's relief there as well. Van Schaick reported that the infant mortality rate had reached as high as four of every ten newborn and the needs of Belgian mothers and children in the unoccupied areas were said to be great.[28] Park decided to send Mabel, Rotholz, and a Belgian nurse as a team to survey conditions in the field and to conduct several clinics. Mabel remembered "When we were ordered to Belgium, van Schaick went off in the Red Cross automobile car with one nurse and his wife dressed in veils as a nurse, while we had to go by train back to Paris and then up, a long trip." They traveled for a month near the front in Flanders visiting rural Belgian villages in the vicinity of Ypres. They discovered that the necessity for relief was not what they were led to believe by Belgians. Van Schaick resurfaced in Mabel Wilcox's letters and diary as an unreliable, feckless official. She wrote of her frustrations, "Came up thinking there was tremendous need up here and that we would have many, many sick children, and that from the 1st of Sept we would care for all new born children in the district assigned to us." Rather, she reported,

> We have found that very few of our people are refugees and that most of them are in better circumstances than they ever have been before – many of them are waxing fat on little shops selling tobacco, chocolates etc to the soldiers or washing for the soldiers, while they all draw a small allowance from the Govt. Most of them have goats and use goats milk for their babies – so the condensed milk is just graft … Some of our villages had had consultations for normal children which we were asked to continue. We found that at these consultations the mothers brot the children had them weighed and then were given 2 or 3 tins of condensed milk and some clothes – easy to see why they came.[29]

She and others disapproved of the civilian hoarding and noted at "one house we went to today the mother received 3 cans a week & was giving the baby cow's milk – so we wanted to find out what happened to the con. milk." She discovered the household busy making a large quantity of cakes for sale to nearby soldiers. "And so it goes," she wrote. "Always the same story of the Belgians – They are after all they can get." She concluded,

> We have had so few sick children and only one new born so far in Sept & found that there are Belgian Drs. in most of our villages, that after a month's survey we shall probably recommend that another area be given us, or that we give up the idea of work up here.[30]

The region was made up of small villages and outlying farms, and the lack of health education in sanitation and infection troubled the team. When Mabel and the others did come upon mothers with sick babies and children, they often were not welcomed. In one case,

L'Emprunt de la Libération

WWI Poster collected by Mabel Wilcox
"L 'Emprunt de la Libération" (The Liberation Loan)
Color Lithograph by artist Abel Faivre
Paris: Imp. Pichot, [1918]
Illustration: The allied flags bearing down on Kaiser Wilheim II

Mabel reported,

> Mother of 5 children – all sickly – dirty & untidy baby locked in room crying – mother digging potatoes, girl of 9 supposed to care for baby … clothes & food & flies all over rooms – baby's milk full of flies. Mother arrived & resented our coming – asking us to leave & never return.

Mabel was near the front as the final Allied offensive of the war began. "We are all hoping that the war is ending & our way," she wrote from Belgium.

> For a week or so we knew it was coming, ammunition was moved up towards the front, the camps of soldiers were emptied overnight and Belgian khaki uniforms giving place to the blue of the French.[31]

There was a tense feeling of excitement, she said, once the artillery shelling commenced and continued for several days. Mabel said, "Dr. R. had helmet but we didn't. One night we were bombed, crawled under bed, two of us trying to get into one helmet. Scared. Planes coming near, then off again."

As the front line of Allied troops advanced into Belgium, the team completed its survey. Returning to Le Havre, Mabel volunteered to be sent back to the front to do military hospital nursing during the final offensive. However, Bicknell wanted her to remain as head nurse at Salle Franklin and manage the work to be done in the city. In fact, the largest number of children were treated in October 1918 at the dispensary and the well-baby clinics. It was reported that,

> Many poor residents of Le Havre are treated now as well as refugees, making it conceivable that with the cessation of the war the work begun here may be spread not only by means of the Belgian aid[e]s into Belgium, but also that it may continue to be of real value to the inhabitants of the French city which gave it birth.[32]

After Armistice Day, the Red Cross began the transfer of Salle Franklin to government and voluntary French authorities. Mabel and Ethel were in Paris on leave at the time of the armistice, and she wrote:

> I had the good fortune to be on a vacation in Paris on Armistice Day. At 11 o'clock in the morning the cannon gave notice that the Armistice was signed, and at that sound, all of Paris went wild. The streets were crowded in a few minutes with people, young and old, rich and poor, walking, dancing, marching, riding in autos, trucks and any sort of conveyance available, all singing the Marseilles and waving flags, showing by their spontaneous enthusiasm and happiness that the most wonderful day of the world the day of glory had come.

German army helmet collected by Mabel Wilcox at the front after Armistice Day.

Medal of Appreciation presented to Mabel by the Queen of Belgium.

Medal of Appreciation presented to Mabel by Mayor of Le Havre on behalf of the city of Le Havre.

They returned to Le Havre to help the French take over. The private charitable organizations of the city, joined by the government, raised funds and made Salle Franklin a permanent institution. The American staff was decorated by the Mayor of Le Havre and by the Queen of Belgium for their service. Park, Rotholz, Wilcox, and Damon were remembered in testimony given by French public health officials:

> By your enterprising spirit, your method and your deep faith in the good to be done, you have created an institution which, I can assure you, will survive your departure from Le Havre. The idea of this work, which has long been in the minds of physicians, the public health workers and the philanthropists of Le Havre, has hitherto, for lack of cooperation, of funds and of support from the authorities, failed of realization.

> You, a foreigner, with the powerful American Red Cross behind you, overcame the first obstacles, and although in the beginning somewhat skeptical, we soon joined you enthusiastically in the project, which assured the fulfillment of all our wishes. Of this, the essential points are the permanent establishment at the dispensary of detailed, careful and repeated examinations to be supplemented with house visits by your public health nurses, who enter firmly, but tactfully, the very heart of the city's misery, the *Quartier St. Francois*, which has been until now an unexplored field of the charitable organizations of Le Havre. You have succeeded completely and in a very short time, in spite of the considerable difficulties which were bound to obstruct your path as they had ours. We have your

example before us. And like you, we are determined no longer to be checked in our work and in our progress.[33]

Mabel commented later, "The French requested Dr. Park to write up procedures, appointment system, etc. Dr. Park had to return to Hopkins." Rotholz, Mabel and the others from Johns Hopkins were left to prepare a detailed written report and Ethel Damon translated it into French.[34] Their report, "The Organization of a Children's Dispensary on the Basis of Appointments for Patients, was published in *Modern Hospital* and in *Archive de Medicine des Enfants* in 1919.

Mabel summarized her thoughts about the role of the Red Cross in public health: "We have in our own civilian populations the same problems that we had in France, the Red Cross has the opportunity to aid the problems of child health and tuberculosis ... for the relief of the suffering, for making the world what the war was fought for, a better place to live." [35] As a nurse in France Mabel saw for herself that Americans were not the only ones addressing infant mortality issues. She witnessed what one historian has called "a virtual explosion of public concern over infant mortality and the consequent emergence of an international welfare movement of truly immense dimensions."

It was during the war years, as Richard Meckel concludes, that the displacement of thousands of people in war-torn Europe created a large population of refugee children, thereby bringing heightened awareness of the needs of maternal and child health care—an awareness that would have a lasting effect on France and other countries. The American Red Cross had brought many physicians, nurses, and social workers into governmental and quasi-governmental service and introduced them to the idea of public health for the first time. Mabel observed in her work how Elizabeth Ashe, Edwards Park, Mason Knox, and other Hopkins staff during the war involved themselves in social and medical reform movements. Their examples affected Mabel's own leadership on Kauai in the following years.[36]

There was another dimension to Mabel's final months in France that climaxed the official recognition she received and her personal autonomy overseas. The many stressful months of caring for the plight of children and mothers and the approaching end to her duty at Salle Franklin had heightened her emotional ties to the French and Belgian children.

In April, 1919 Mabel wrote Elsie, "[W]e are wearing a grey & rose ribbon [the Queen's medal] with considerable pride. There is no gory glory attached to it however." Mabel then added that she, Ethel, a Red Cross nurse from South Africa, and Dr. Rotholz were planning to adopt a baby in Le Havre:

> I hope such news items as a decoration and attachment of 1/4 of a baby won't be too much for the family. Don't worry, I shall not flaunt either in anybody's face—but you will be consumed in admiration. [37]

Mabel told Elsie that Dr. Park had approved of the idea of the adoption and encouraged them to take the baby to the United States. Mabel asked Elsie if she could find a plantation nurse's position or a Mokihana Club position for the Red Cross nurse on Kauai, and they would come to Kauai to nurture the infant, an orphan or abandoned baby.

The thinking changed before they left Le Havre, however, and it was decided that Miss S., the Red Cross nurse, would become the adoptive parent. They made plans to rendezvous with the baby in Massachusetts for several months of rest and relaxation.

The delay in coming home bothered Elsie and her parents and Mabel described the circumstances in the following way to Elsie:

> When Miss S. arrived we thot of going West immediately, but she wasn't in very good condition—has nursed steadily almost all through the war—and she was destitute almost as to clothes having saved every penny to get to Hawaii. ... I'm sorry if you all feel I've done wrong & don't want to come home. I thot I'd worked out the thing to the best for everybody. Without this rest I'm sure Miss S. couldn't have done a year's work. I hope this will come out OK. We will be in S.F. about ten days before our sailing date and I trust that on arrival my sins will be forgiven me!

Two weeks later Mabel wrote Elsie:

> Miss S. has a chance to stay in the East and I had already advised her to take it & keep her few earnings. You may think this queer after having asked you to get her a position, however I think all I need say is, that it is advisable for her to take this work & that Lihue will probably be better off as she knows nothing of American district nursing and would have had to have some help on the job. ... Miss S. will of course keep the baby here—so our party somewhat dwindles. [38]

Chapter Nine

PUBLIC HEALTH IN EVERYDAY
LIFE ON KAUAI

In November 1919, Mabel was welcomed home by her family at Grove Farm and the Mokihana Club honored her with a reception and dance. Mabel spoke at a meeting of Club members about war and her health care experiences. In particular she described the refugees who were "scattered over the whole map of France," especially children between the ages of 5 to 16 who suffered the most because of poor food—the adolescents "were five years behind what they had been."[1] She also spoke to the local schools, and sixty years later Charles Katsumu Tanimoto recalled: "A lovely lady, dressed in all white, came to my class to speak to the children of her experiences as an army nurse in Europe during World War I. She was like the Angel of Mercy in my story book and I fell in love with her."

In 1920 Mabel joined Elsie in selecting Estelle Roe, a trained social worker from Chicago, to work for Grove Farm plantation. Roe's welfare routine centered on living conditions and included many daily home visits, assisting mothers with diets for children, times of meals, minor illnesses, and school truancy prevention. Although she moved to Grove Farm for only a year, she set up a daily nursery as a "play school" in the new Puhi camp, and coached Grove Farm's boys' and girls' sports teams as well as hosting social open houses at a recreation hall every other Saturday night.[2]

Mabel served as probation officer of the Juvenile Court in 1920–21 as the Territorial legislature took up and passed new welfare laws to deal with problems of undernourished children, institutional care of "mentally defective" children, and the staffing of the juvenile court. But Mabel's work on the board of directors of Samuel Mahelona Memorial Hospital, after she accepted appointment by the County Supervisors, was the most important focus of her attention.

The Wilcox family continued to provide leadership at Mahelona. Her brother Charles was also on the Mahelona board, and her Aunt Emma made a substantial donation to expand the sanatorium wards after her husband Albert's death in 1919. Charles, Mabel, and Elsie shared interests in social welfare, education, and the sanatorium, especially after Elsie was appointed Territorial Commissioner for Education for Kauai.[3]

The three of them were in the prime of life and entering a time of maximum personal commitment to Kauai. Charles had taken Ralph's place at Grove Farm. With Edward Broadbent as manager, the plantation had instituted a contract cultivation system and, like other plantations after sugar industry strikes in 1909 and 1920, improved working conditions. Greater mechanization put Grove Farm in the forefront of agricultural technology on the smaller plantations. G. N. Wilcox turned 80 in 1919 and was still actively involved at Grove Farm, making Hawaii and California investments and supporting impressive charitable interests. He was well known in the Islands for his regular gifts to organizations like the Salvation Army, YMCA, YWCA, and private schools and churches.

The family was still recovering from Ralph's death four years earlier, but its misfortunes did not come singly. In June 1920 Charles died in an automobile accident. His car skidded off the Waimea Canyon mountain road, and he and his niece Elizabeth were killed instantly. Charles' wife Marion, their daughter Lois, and a friend were injured.

After the wrenching events of the deaths of the two brothers, Sam and Emma had a parish hall built at the Lihue Church in 1921 as a memorial to Ralph and Charles. Constructed on the church grounds near Grove Farm, the new building, designed by the Honolulu architect Hart Wood, was used for plays, musical recitals, and meetings of the Mokihana Club and other community organizations.[4] Mabel, Elsie, and Etta deepened their sense of their own midlife and became intent on preserving their family history by recording memories of their parents and Uncle George.

Although Mabel's brother Gaylord remained in Honolulu in a management post at American Factors, he accepted G. N.'s request to represent him on important boards on Oahu, and Digby Sloggett was made treasurer of Grove Farm. He and Etta and their children moved back to Kauai from Maui, so the entire Wilcox family could function as a unit. After nearly 60 years of his independent ownership, G. N. made the decision to incorporate Grove Farm. He served as company president, appointed Elsie vice-president and Mabel as secretary. As plantation directors they both were active in improving the welfare of the workforce in housing and public health.[5]

In 1920 Mabel and her sisters began the restoration of Waioli Mission House by first purchasing it from their Uncle Albert's estate and "established it as a Memorial to the Missionaries, Abner and Lucy Eliza Hart Wilcox, a Community House." They had first developed a love of old buildings when they were at school in Massachusetts. Mabel and Elsie visited their great-grandfather's farm homestead in Harwinton, Connecticut with their Uncle Edward and enjoyed seeing many examples of historic preservation. The sisters realized that the old Waioli Mission property where their father and his brothers were raised in Hanalei had a meaning and purpose beyond themselves. It is the earliest historic house museum restoration in Hawaii. Mabel, Elsie, and Etta asked Ethel Damon to interview Sam and G. N. and she wrote a history of the Waioli Mission Station for *The Friend*, the publication of the Hawaiian Mission Children's Society.

In 1922 Elsie and Ethel went "antiquing" in New England, selecting additional bed, chests, chairs and rugs for Waioli.

G. N. treated Ethel as a member of his family. He was concerned about her welfare and in 1920 he made her a present of C. Brewer & Co. stock. Mabel wrote Ethel:

> He said he was having a fine time giving away his property; that not many men lived long enough to enjoy being able to do so. Then he said he didn't know anyone he would rather give to than you, because you "belonged to our crowd," and he felt you would make good use of it.

Ethel acknowledged G. N.'s gift, telling him, "This makes it possible for me to study Hawaiian among Hawaiians as I could not have hoped to do otherwise."

The Wilcoxes visited Waioli often, and it became their family refuge. Etta and Digby's son Richard remembered how much it meant to them to find a large collection of letters of Abner and Lucy stored away in the Waioli parlor bookcase along with his great-grandparents' devotional and historical library and Hawaiian language schoolbooks. The restoration of Waioli was more than the preservation of just the family's old home, however. Elsie wrote "some of the land is now an open Common. We want to convert that into a play-ground and park for Community use," and they continued to lease acreage behind the house in the Waioli Valley to support irrigated wetland taro farming, something that continues until this day.[6]

Mabel spent the next few years involved in Mahelona Hospital's organization and the expansion of its services and staff. As the number of tuberculosis cases at sanatoria on Kauai, Oahu, Maui, and Hawaii continued to grow, people accepted the fact that the sanatorium was not a *make* house, a place for the living dead. Physicians and nurses alike had developed confidence in the restorative powers of tuberculosis hospitals and were devoted to the healing that took place in the systematic rest care activities of infected patients. Tuberculosis remained a leading health problem in Hawaii, but except for surgical lung treatment, there were no alternatives to rest cure until the drug use of revolutionary antibiotics was worked out in the 1950s. Patients at Mahelona and other sanatoria were admitted with active lesions in their lungs and associated lymph nodes resulting from the infection of the pulmonary tissue in one or both lungs with tuberculosis bacillus. The rest cure, scheduled exercise, and diet were critical in healing the lesions to help patients build up their resistance and immunity to further infection. It was expected that a patient whose case was arrested by this treatment would be kept segregated at Mahelona three to six months and then allowed to leave with stationary or retrogressive lesions, but it was soon discovered that the average length of isolation at Mahelona needed to be two to five years, and some unimproved patients spent practically the rest of their lives there. There were more infected persons to be found, and the hospital remained filled to capacity.[7]

As Mabel, the other directors, and nurses concentrated on good care, one insider's reminiscences in the 1980s complement official hospital reports of sixty years earlier and describe the feelings of a patient about how his day was routinized, month after month.[8] Mahelona became Lawrence Ferreiro's world for more than a dozen years. He recalled,

> When they told you had TB, it seemed as though the earth was just about ready to open and swallow you. ... I put in 13 years at Mahelona, 13 years on the shelf. I was 20 years old when I entered the hospital.
>
> You see in those days when you went to Mahelona it was something like you were condemned to die. The whole philosophy at that time was: 'Here is a place to go to and wait to die.' There was no medication at that time for tuberculosis.
>
> Early homesickness was inevitable: When your parents told you, 'You go,' you went. So I went to Mahelona. It's alright. For a while. For the first couple of weeks, it was really bad. Down and out.

Mentally it's something. ... Of course, now it's another thing. Now tuberculosis is just like an ordinary cold, but at that time you feel dejected and rejected and everything else.

The daily routine? Morning breakfast like everybody else a little after seven o'clock. Then the nurses come in and bathe you. Usually it's not a nurse. It's a maid. Rest period from nine-thirty about to ten-thirty. Of course, when you have your rest period you can read. I had a brother who had a little magazine stand in town to make some extra money. Every month we'd see what is not sold. Those magazines come on consignment. In those days they had to rip off the cover and send it back to the distributor on Oahu to get credit for the magazines that were not sold. So I had a wide variety of materials.

Then you have lunch about eleven o'clock from there on a little while. Then, one, two, three, you rest again. Everybody is supposed to try to sleep. Even the ambulatory patients, they try to keep them in bed. But in my case like I was in a private room. It was hard to control, see. I was in bed. I used this excuse. I told the nurses a lot of time, 'I cannot sleep.' I was on those sleeping pills there for a long time.

After three o'clock then you have dinner at four-thirty. Then after that it's visiting ... from three to four you have visiting hours. Then after six o'clock visiting hours till eight o'clock. During my time we had a lot of programs. Stage shows, magicians, and everything they could grab hold of. We had a movie show every week. Other shows, people, school groups used to come entertain; singing, and play-acting. They'd wheel my bed out. I had a brother who was quite a boxer, and he was a school teacher here. He trained a few boxers to play with the amateur fights. I used to fool around with them when I was in school. He brought these boys up, these high school boys. They came up there special for me. Had a little boxing exhibition out on the lawn. They moved my bed outside.

We had good people there working, too. The nurses used to come. Oh yes. They were wonderful. The Wilcox family did a wonderful thing to put that up there to take care of the people here on this island.[9]

Ferreiro healed. He was discharged from Mahelona, took a job as a sports announcer and lived for many more years.

Mabel and others saw that the early detection of tuberculosis was as important as ever, and even with the increasing number of hospitalized patients at Mahelona, case finding was a persistent, difficult problem. There were several reasons for this. As the Territorial Board of Health's Clara Figeley, R.N., noted, "If communicable disease is to be controlled it must be by securing the confidence of the mother or other responsible head of the family and demonstrating to such a one how disease may be prevented—in other words, practical demonstration must take the place of precept." This was more difficult than it seemed because many families were still reluctant to report tuberculosis. As one of Mahelona's nurses, Miyoko Ednaco, R.N., remembered, "They didn't find them because everybody used to hide that they had TB, mostly the Japanese. … TB was one disease that in Japanese life, why it was terrible to have TB, and Filipinos too, they'd work you know, till they're bad and then they'll come to the hospital."[10]

Board of Health and sanatoria nurses continued to appeal to physicians to report tuberculosis cases as soon as they diagnosed them. Figeley told a meeting of the Medical Society of Hawaii, "Do not think that because the case is an advanced one that it need not be reported because someone else has surely done so. … In the meantime the patient lives among his family infecting his young children through carelessness or ignorance."[11] A meeting of all Kauai physicians held in 1923 at Mahelona considered ways and means of finding and hospitalizing more people infected with tuberculosis. At the suggestion of Mabel and her brother-in-law Digby, who was appointed Mahelona's part-time manager after Charles' death, the need to secure a permanent, full-time, resident tuberculosis doctor at Mahelona was

Lihue School Health Fair showing students attacking the "tuberculosis dragon".

*Mabel Wilcox's Territorial
nurse's uniform.*

brought up to the directors. Mabel believed that a full-time physician would conduct regularly scheduled, free diagnostic clinics around the island and increase the number of patients to be treated. Arthur W. Duryea, M.D., was engaged by the directors in 1925. He was a graduate of the College of Physicians and Surgeons at Columbia University, had recently completed a residency in the tuberculosis division at Bellevue Hospital in New York. He has also practiced in sanatoria at Saranac Lake, New York, the center of tuberculosis care on the East Coast.[12]

With Duryea on Kauai, Mahelona gave more free physical diagnoses in the plantation hospitals at Lihue, Koloa, Makaweli, Eleele, and Waimea, as well as at the Kapaa Armory. The purpose of the clinics was to detect the disease in its early stages and improve chances for a patient's successful hospitalization. The clinics drew on the case-finding help of three new Board of Health nurses: Clarisa Bromley, Florence Geyer, and Mrs. Glaisyer. People were examined who had contact with known tubercular cases, and many undernourished children were identified in schools and camps. Within the year, the clinics tested nearly 600 individuals, and of these 45 were admitted to Mahelona.[13]

Duryea moved to Honolulu the following year, however, but the directors replaced him with F. J. Leman, M.D., Leman continued the clinics on a semi-monthly basis.

In 1925 the Territorial Board of Health invited Mabel to return to fulltime public health nursing and to take charge of a groundbreaking new Federal program of maternal child nursing and health education. She accepted the position as Kauai's first Territorial Maternity and Infant Hygiene Nurse. In a further step, she then was made Supervising Child Hygiene Nurse and put in charge of a staff of the three public health nurses—Bromley, Geyer, and Glaisyer—who worked out of her cottage office at Grove Farm.

Based upon her experience at Mahelona and with the Mokihana Club and her familiarity with voluntary associations such as Palama Settlement, Mabel believed that by bringing families and individuals into contact with the health care resources of the community, nurses could become mediators. It seems likely that Mabel accepted the Board of Health staff position because it was an opportunity to address the urgent need in Hawaii for additional personnel to reduce infant and maternal mortality and to improve diet and nutrition for women and children. She had witnessed that the widespread lack of trained public health nurses held back community health efforts, and her appointment was a chance to extend access to care and strengthen the reciprocal relationships of voluntary and government services.

Before Mabel took up her new Territorial duties she took a vacation with Ethel Damon, cousin Helen Lyman, and Mary Alder, a friend of hers. They visited Japan, Egypt, Italy, and France.

The new public health services were made possible in the Islands by matching funds appropriated by the U.S. Congress after passage of the Sheppard-Towner Act in 1921, America's first federal social welfare legislation.[14] The Territorial Board of Health had ongoing financial responsibilities for the hospitalization of leprosy, tuberculosis, and mentally ill patients, and with the new Sheppard-Towner funds, the board hired its first pediatrician, increased the size of the public health nursing staff, and organized clinics on each island for mothers and infants.

Vivia B. Appleton, M.D., was selected by the Board of Health in 1925 to take charge of implementation of the program authorized by the Federal Act for the Promotion of the Welfare and Hygiene of Maternity and Infancy. She picked Kauai to become the first health center demonstration project in Hawaii because Kauai was small in size and had a moderate number of annual births—about 1,200 a year in 1925—and because she knew Mabel as the most experienced public health nurse outside of Honolulu. Appleton was familiar with the work of the Mokihana Club, where she had been a speaker.

Palama Settlement nurse providing infant and maternal care in plantation camp house on Oahu. c. 1925 (Photo courtesy Palama Settlement)

Appleton had been trained at Johns Hopkins Medical School. Before the First World War she taught pediatrics at the University of California as an assistant to William P. Lucas, M.D. During the war she served with the Red Cross Children's Bureau in France when Lucas was appointed its director, and she was sent to Brittany to set up a child welfare program. Her wartime experience with civilian public health was similar to Mabel's. Appleton also had medical experience in such diverse places as Labrador and China. As the stepdaughter of a U.S. Attorney for Hawaii, she came to Honolulu after doctoring Chinese children in Shanghai and researching nutrition for the Council on Health Education in China.[15]

Implementation of the Sheppard-Towner Act, like the anti-tuberculosis campaign, was another turning point in public health in Hawaii. Budgeted funds helped extend free community services to new and prospective Hawaiian mothers as well as to the plantations, where there were numerous recently arrived immigrant Filipino wives. Although the program did not replace existing, traditional home-birthing practices and midwivery, it complemented plantation medicine and the contributions of the voluntary social service organizations. At the new Territorial well-baby clinics and conferences, women were taught about maternity and infant and child health, diet, and nutrition.

Territorial "Well-Baby Clinic" photo illustrating that a breast-fed baby is healthier than bottle-fed baby. c. 1925

The newborn and school-age children were regularly weighed and examined by public health nurses and plantation physicians.

The reduction of infant mortality was a positive result of the Sheppard-Towner Act nationally. On the mainland, Sheppard-Towner provided access to public health care for black women and children, Native Americans, and Hispanics, many of whom had been ignored by public health departments; the program's concern was with the unequal distribution of maternal and child health care, and its spirit was egalitarian.

In Hawaii, the goal was access to new public health centers for all women of childbearing age. Appleton stated that the Board of Health sought "the prevention of maternal and infant mortality and the promotion of the health and welfare of little children from conception through infancy and the pre-school period up to school age." She said the mission was to "save the lives of hundreds of babies likely to be undernourished or exposed to disease" and "to save the lives of mothers who may be endangered because of lack of care."

It was Mabel's responsibility to make efficient use of the new resources. After the first ten months under her supervision, the demonstration centers on Kauai had an attendance of 4,403 mothers, infants, and children, and nearly 1,000 home visits had been made by the nurses assigned to her.[16] Some mothers had to be coaxed to attend, but it was estimated that as many as 50 percent of all Kauai infants under one year of age had been enrolled at the clinics, an impressive result.

By 1926 there were as many as 17 well-baby centers on Kauai. Nine were administered by the Division of Maternal and Child Hygiene with Sheppard-Towner funds and the others were run by the plantations. As their activities increased, infant mortality on Kauai decreased, dropping by approximately 14 percent in the first year. Appleton reported that throughout the Territory 32 percent of Hawaiian children and 26 percent of Filipino children born in 1926 were enrolled in the clinics. "The amount of work done in the second year was almost double that of the first year," she wrote. Appleton pointed out that Filipino and Hawaiian infants had the greatest mortality. "While the clinics will be open to all persons, emphasis will be placed at first on the education of Filipina and Hawaiian mothers," she said.[17]

Mabel understood the need for bilingual nurses. The Mokihana nurse, Vera Marston, R.N., reported the problem:

> Perhaps the most difficult problem is with the Filipinos. Their living conditions are worse than those of the other races and they are contented with less. … In spite of this much could be done for their general health and the feeding of the babies. It is very hard to converse. … If it was possible to get the assistance of a Filipino nurse, much could be done for them. Many babies could be saved if the parents could understand. The Filipinos have not been in-different and they are always glad to have the nurse come to see them. There are several families buying cow's milk which they can ill afford but are doing so because the nurse said it was necessary for the babies health.[18]

There were several Filipina plantation nurses at Makaweli and Kilauea, but the only trained public health nurse on Kauai from the Philippines was Josefina Cortezan. She arrived at Koloa in 1923 with her husband, who was the minister of the Koloa Union Church, and began home visiting and prenatal care for Koloa Sugar Co. Cortezan had been trained in Manila at the Mary J. Johnston Hospital School of Nursing and had later worked at a public health center in the Philippines and at Palama Settlement in Honolulu. She also had been a visiting nurse at Ewa Plantation on Oahu. Because Cortezan was not a United States citizen, she could not be hired by the Territory as a public health nurse. To circumvent this restriction, Mabel asked the Kauai Y.W.C.A. to hire her in 1926 as its visiting nurse.[19]

Cortezan worked closely with other nurses on Kauai, but the Secretary of the Board of the Hawaiian Evangelical Association, Norman C. Schenck, wrote to the Kauai Y.W.C.A. protesting the arrangement of hiring the minister's wife. His response was typical of many prevailing attitudes towards working wives who were also mothers. Elsie was angered by the letter, and backing up Mabel, she wrote Schenck:

> I understand that the Hawaiian Board is paying Mrs. Cortezan no salary and has no claim on her other than that which any church or community has upon the wife of its pastor. The day has long since gone by when a woman was so much a part of her husband that she could not establish a separate individuality—and vice versa. You, for instance, are at perfect liberty to employ Mr. Matsuura, the husband of our Japanese YW worker. We have no claim on him.
>
> As you know, it is almost impossible to secure good Filipino workers. We must use what is available, and it seems far and away the best thing for Mrs. Cortezan, who is a fine influence, to extend her work as far as possible. At present Mrs. Cortezan's work is all planned for, the backing of Plantation managers secured, etc., and we cannot withdraw without great detriment to the respect in which our work is held. Also, I think we ought not to withdraw when I consider the work to be done. ... I beg you not to intimidate our worker.[20]

Cortezan, who worked along the lines of this practical arrangement for many years, recalled:

> So, they put up the Wilcox trust fund money to pay me so I can help with the Filipino workers and I covered the whole island to help with the Filipino workers and I covered the whole island to help with the mothers, advise them and then go to the hospital. That's why some people said, 'How do you know all these people?' And I say, 'Well I work with them long ago when they had their babies.'[21]

Appleton believed that the efforts to reach Filipino families were not as difficult as locating Hawaiians. "There are less than six hundred Hawaiian births a year," she wrote, "So it is necessary to work in some of the more sparsely populated districts in order to reach a larger proportion of Hawaiians to meet their infant mortality."[22]

Appleton visited Puna and Kona on the Big Island to investigate health conditions among Hawaiians, and she remarked about their humanity.

> People told me that the Hawaiian mothers wouldn't follow directions for the care of their babies and selves. I have found that this is wrong. Hawaiian mothers are just as easy to deal with—and are just as anxious to find out how to properly care for babies as are the mothers of any other race.[23]

On Kauai nurses and plantation doctors came to the clinics only equipped with scales, record forms, and weight books for babies, and with this simple collection they went to work. Umeyo Tamashiro recalled one of the nurses:

> She really helped. She came in as soon as we are pregnant we let her know. Then we used to go in and check monthly. Weigh ourselves. They had an armory, Kapaa Armory. They had a special room for us. For pregnant mothers and babies. She used to come to the house to help wash the babies. We used to ask her what we didn't know. She used to explain everything to us.[24]

As more and more infants and children were brought to the health centers under the Sheppard-Towner program, one public health specialist wrote,

"Whose Baby is 00?" print hanging on the wall of Mabel Wilcox's public health nursing office at Grove Farm.

The well baby conferences are largely educational. Parents bring infants and young children to the centers for weighing, measuring and a private interview with the physician who advises as to normal growth and development (both physical and mental), including diet, sunbaths, cod liver oil, correct habits of hygiene, and the like. The importance of smallpox vaccination and of diphtheria immunization is emphasized, especially during the first year.[25]

Describing the influence of the clinics on the west side of Kauai, Edith Nicholson, R.N., said:

After about five years, there was a very sudden improvement in feeding, nutrition and immunization just nagging, and visiting them all the time and encouraging them to do all these things.[26]

The Board of Health's Division of Maternal and Infant program on Kauai rapidly expanded under Appleton and Mabel. Appleton reported that, "Babies born this year on the islands have a better chance of living and being healthy than they have had [in a] previous year." Attendance at the well-baby clinics on Kauai continued to climb, and in 1927 they treated 8,398 mothers and infants. The percentage of infants under supervision on Kauai reached 85 percent, which was a rate higher than any other island. Appleton said of Kauai, "The infant mortality rate was the lowest rate ever held in the Territory of any county or city." She concluded that, "It is perfectly possible to reduce infant mortality, but it requires an expert knowledge of the underlying principles of pediatrics."[27]

Some years later Mabel Smyth, R.N., who succeeded Appleton in directing the Territory's maternal and infant care nurses, summarized Mabel Wilcox's special skills in public health nursing:

More now than in former years the health work carried on by Miss Wilcox brings her into close contact with people of many races. Where the rural public health formerly involved chiefly Hawaiian and Chinese families, with a few of Anglo-Saxon or German combinations, racial groupings now include Japanese, Korean, Portuguese, Filipino and Porto Rican. An instinctive understanding of many personal problems of adjustment as well as of physical health is supplemented by years of experience in the sympathetic viewpoint which Miss Wilcox brings to bear upon her work. [28]

Elizabeth Fee, in her study of the professionalization of public health in the United States during these years, defines public health in terms of its goal of reducing disease and maintaining the health of the population. Considering these aims, Mabel's achievements in tuberculosis and maternal and child health care on Kauai was an exceptional case history. She was the hub of the island's public health programs.

Chapter Ten

COLLABORATION AND CONFLICT

The decade of the 1920s was "a special moment in the history of public health nursing," historian Karen Buhler-Wilkerson observes of the field in the United States, as trained nurses like Mabel played key roles in tackling the interrelated problems of infant mortality, nutrition, and the persistence of contagious diseases like tuberculosis, reaching out through clinics and house visits.

The popularity of the new programs resulted in understaffing and administrative problems, however, exposing conflicts and the need for more effective leadership and planning to integrate services. These needs brought help from the Honolulu United Welfare Fund which enlisted the assistance of the American Public Health Association. The coalition formed a local advisory committee made up of Honolulu business, social services, medical and educational leaders. They realized that the public interest would be served best by the preparation of a long-range plan for the Board of Health by an outside authority. Professor Ira V. Hiscock of the Department of Public Health at Yale University, who was also a member of the New Haven Board of Health, was invited by the American Public Health Association to work with the *ad hoc* advisory committee. When Hiscock's *A Survey of Health and Welfare Activities in Honolulu, Hawaii* was completed in 1929, it became the Board of Health's program blueprint and plan for requests for budgets for the Territory.

Hiscock's conclusions were sobering but not unexpected. He wrote that "this appraisal result means that the combined totals of Honolulu official and voluntary services (including Territorial) measures only a little over half the score of the best examples of such services in other cities of comparable size." Hiscock had conducted similar surveys for other large communities on the mainland, and his objectivity and knowledge of the staffing and administrative needs of a well-organized public health agency were well respected.

Social service advocates had been trying to create a broader understanding of community health needs throughout the 1920s. Palama Settlement, new annual Territorial Conferences on Social Work, and the Hawaii Territorial Medical Association shared professional experiences even before federal aid from the Sheppard-Towner Act reached Hawaii.

Palama Settlement's head nurse, Mabel Smyth, took the lead in professional meetings by discussing duties of public health nurses and the mutual relationships of trained nurses, social workers, physicians, and sugar plantation industrial relations supervisors. At the First Territorial Conference on Social Work in 1921, Smyth explained that the public health nurse "may be an Island Welfare nurse, a School nurse, a Medical Social Service nurse, a Tuberculosis nurse, an Industrial nurse, a Plantation nurse, a District or Visiting nurse, or if she were working in a small community or in a rural district, she may combine these functions."[1]

Another participant in the First Territorial Conference was Vivia Appleton, a few years before she joined the Board of Health staff. At the meeting she spoke about "An Ounce of Prevention"—a phrase that would become commonplace in speaking about public health— and observed that "preventive medicine works along two lines: the combative, which is against disease; and the encouraging of life."[2]

Smyth had discussed the relationship between public health nurses and physicians at the Annual meeting of the Medical Society of Hawaii in 1924, where several physicians expressed their lack of familiarity with public health nursing. A. N. Sinclair, M.D., the early leader in the anti-tuberculosis campaign in Hawaii, said, "I am surprised to learn of the functions of the district nurse. I myself did not know of them." Paul Withington, M.D., noted, "I would like to have it made known who the district nurses are and where they can be found outside of Palama. There is no question as to their absolute value and need." Bertie Mobbs, M.D., added, "I agree with both Dr. Withington and Dr. Sinclair. The district nurse is a great help in preventing children with communicable diseases from attending school. The trouble is that the average Doctor does not know where he can get in touch with these nurses when he wants them. There should be more publicity."[3]

The theme of A. N. Sinclair's President's Address to the Hawaii Territorial Medical Association in 1927 was the need for increased cooperation among physicians and between doctors and "organizations whose interests and activities are related to public health or to the sick." Sinclair cited mutual cooperation between the Board of Health and private physicians as "one of the most important that the medical profession can consider." Based on his experience with tuberculosis, Sinclair drew attention to those physicians who neglected to notify the Board of Health in cases of contagious diseases.[4] Sinclair's message pointed to one of the problems sociologist Paul Starr describes in *The Social Transformation of American Medicine:*

> Extending the boundaries of public health to incorporate more of medicine seemed necessary and desirable to some public health officials, but as one might imagine, private practitioners regarded such extensions as a usurpation. Doctors fought against public treatment of the sick, requirements for reporting cases of tuberculosis and venereal disease, and attempts by public health authorities to establish health centers to coordinate preventive and curative medical services.[5]

A transition to generalized public health nursing was underway in the 1920s in Hawaii. While Mabel was in France, Elsie had written to Dora Isenberg in 1918 and suggested a second public health nurse for Kauai to the Board of Health. "Let the Tuberculosis Nurse do school work dividing up the two jobs ... both school & tuberculosis work, one from Lihue to Haena, the other on the Waimea side. ... Mabel always thought the work should be combined & worked out in this way."

As health education and social welfare developed in Hawaii, Margaret Bergen provided the Territorial Conferences on Social Work with historical and personal insights from her groundbreaking social work in London, mainland cities, as well as at the Associated Charities in Honolulu. Bergen had also led the Board of Health's organization of a public health nursing course at the University of Hawaii in 1926, attended by nurses from the Board of Health and Palama Settlement.[6]

Bergen acted as a mentor to Elsie and Mabel, and in 1921 Elsie had written to her about the organization of social services on Kauai, describing plantation hospitals, recreational facilities, programs of the YMCA and YWCA, and problems of malnutrition. Social workers spoke at the Territorial Conferences on the subject of nutrition: Estelle Roe from Grove Farm had tested differences among unmarried Filipino workers who were eating at plantation camp boarding houses compared to those who provided their own food and cooked in camp houses. She described the favorable results of the boarding house meals. Clinton Childs from the Alexander House Settlement on Maui talked about problems of underweight school children. Public awareness of malnutrition broadened after 1923 when the Territorial Legislature appropriated funds to the Board of Education for a Nutrition Department and program of health education in the schools.

After the Legislature accepted the provisions of the Sheppard-Towner Act and the board established the Divisions of Maternal and Infant Hygiene, Appleton was hired as the board's full-time physician in charge—the board's first pediatrician and female doctor. Both Trotter and Appleton mentioned a "spirit of cooperation" in their annual reports. Trotter called attention to national public health nursing standards emphasizing the "special personal qualifications that are desirable for all public health nurses—adaptability, tact, patience, tolerance, courtesy, a spirit of cooperation and an open mind." Appleton, who had chosen her new staff of supervisory nurses, including Mabel Wilcox, sounded optimistic as she looked back on her first year's work.[7]

But what did not appear in the annual report was a growing management conflict among Trotter, President of the Board of Health, Board of Health members, and Appleton.

Trouble first broke out over whether Appleton, who had been on the staff of the University of California Medical School, should obtain a license to practice medicine in the Territory. Appleton did not feel she needed to be licensed, objecting on the grounds that conducting her clinic consultations with children and mothers was strictly educational and diagnostic.

Trotter stated that he considered Appleton "very competent in her knowledge of infancy and maternity work, but that she had an idea that this activity was of the greatest importance and that every other detail under the Board of Health should be subservient to her work." He added, "[S]he has apparently never worked in a large department before and does not apparently realize that her usefulness and results to be obtained can only result from cooperation and assistance from others of the Board of Health."[8]

Trotter and Appleton were nearly the same age and both were experienced in public medicine. Trotter had over 25 years in government service as a quarantine officer at federal posts in Florida, Cuba, and California before coming to Hawaii in 1912 as the Territory's

Chief Quarantine Officer. During the Spanish American War he was an Army surgeon and also understood tropical medicine and the control of epidemics and communicable diseases. Like many other health officers of the time, however, his education and background lacked knowledge of the maternal and infant welfare movement.[9]

Appleton's working relationship with Mabel had been a good one. They each wrote to Trotter to obtain permission to attend a Washington D.C. conference, for example, and when these plans did not materialize, Appleton requested, and the board agreed, that Mabel come to Honolulu to supervise the division while Appleton attended the conference. There was growing staff friction between Clara Figeley, the Board of Health's Supervisor of Public Health Nursing, and Appleton over the question of which division would have charge of staff nurses if the board adopted a generalized public health nursing plan. Figeley's 1927 report brought their differences to a head when Appleton called attention to duplicated figures for cases under the supervision of tuberculosis nurses "in defense of a continued program which makes tuberculosis nursing the prime work of the public health nurses of the Board of Health."[10]

In 1927, during a six-week absence of Trotter on the mainland while he attended meetings and recruited a physician for the tuberculosis division, Appleton discussed what she considered to be Figeley's inflated figures for tuberculosis nursing cases with Charles B. Cooper, M.D., a member of the board. Cooper was the board's former commissioner and president from 1904 to 1919, and he chaired the board committee Trotter had appointed more than a year earlier to make recommendations for merging tuberculosis and school nurses under the supervision of Appleton's Bureau of Maternity and Infant Hygiene. Cooper and the other two board members on the subcommittee were impatient. At the board meeting on May 18, Cooper discussed the disputed figures and said, "This simply means a duplication of work and a good deal of friction. Why should the Child Hygiene work be reported to the Tuberculosis Bureau, as it is none of their business."

On June 9, the board went into executive session and the subcommittee reported:

> In the interest of economy, harmony and efficiency, we deem it advisable to have all nurses engaged in Maternal and Child Hygiene or Public Health and School operate under the supervision of one head. With this end in view we have provided that all nurses employed in tuberculosis or schoolwork shall carry on their duties under the supervision of the Bureau of Maternity and Infant Hygiene.[11]

When Trotter met the board on July 20, he objected to the reorganization of the public health nurses under Appleton's direction. He presented a plan that he had worked out with several other members of the board: He would agree to the reorganization, accept Figeley's resignation from her position, but Appleton would have to be dismissed because of alleged lack of harmony in his staff. He discussed letters from several plantation physicians and a manager about disagreements with the Maternal and Infant Bureau.

The board minutes show the dilemma the members faced with Trotter. One member said he wanted to go on record that it was unfortunate to terminate "such an eminent and efficient health executive" as Appleton. He thought it would disrupt the bureau to "let personality enter into this." However, another member said he felt the board should back Trotter "in any matter affecting the personnel." When the vote was taken about Appleton it was unanimously agreed to support Trotter's recommendation to dismiss her. However, the board reiterated that the reorganization should move forward and that someone should be appointed to take Appleton's place before she left the board in August. Trotter said that he would bring the supervising Maternal and Infant Hygiene nurse from Hilo to Honolulu. Trotter's suggestion was unacceptable to the board.[12]

It is not known where the idea originated for appointing Mabel Smyth to fill Appleton's position, but the record of a special meeting held on July 26 read:

> Dr. Trotter stated that he had considered the matter of a chief for the Bureau of Maternity and Infancy and had found a person well qualified, in his opinion, for the position, namely Miss Mabel Smyth, Head Nurse at the Palama Settlement. She had agreed to accept this position, provided that Mr. Rath gave his consent to allow her to terminate her services at the Palama Settlement. Dr. Trotter said that he had consulted with

Copy of portrait of Mabel Smythe, R.N. which Mabel Wilcox put in the Grove Farm house.

Mr. Rath, Head Worker of the Palama Settlement, and he readily gave his consent.[13]

Mabel Wilcox seriously considered resigning her Board of Health position over the firing of Appleton. When she learned that Trotter had asked Mabel Smyth at Palama Settlement to take Appleton's place she reconsidered, and Smyth tried to reassure Mabel: "I do feel very keenly about this whole affair—because I know the board and Dr. Trotter have completely lost sight of this fact that the community has lost a very efficient doctor and splendid woman by letting Dr. Appleton go."[15] Appleton, who remained in Honolulu, went into private practice as a pediatrician.

Mabel Smyth wrote to Mabel Wilcox:

There is only one thing I can do Mabel and that is that I will try and get the nurses together and keep up what has already been established and work towards getting [another] full time physician who will tie up their medical work.

I fully appreciate your friendship and respect and admiration for Dr. Appleton and all she has done and stood for in her work in the community. Mere words alone cannot express my appreciation to you for reconsidering and staying on with the work. Mabel *we*

Mabel Wilcox's public health nurses' office and library at Grove Farm.

must have you to tie up the whole of Kauai, for you are the only one who can do it especially at this critical time.

Mabel Smyth wrote after a visit to Kauai: "Somehow Mabel I feel so much better about the whole situation and the future of our work." The two eventually saw eye to eye, but it was years before Trotter appointed another full-time physician. A year later Smyth wrote that "the rock upon which we have built this division is the health center," adding that "the degree of success we have had in these centers arises largely from the cooperation of plantation managers, doctors and nurses, government doctors, Board of Health nurses, the working members of the various social agencies, and numerous public-spirited laymen."[15]

It was impossible for the Board of Health administration to ignore the success of the Sheppard-Towner program, and the local clinics clearly demonstrated the value of preventive medicine and its contributions to the downward trend in infant mortality.

Smyth, who regarded Mabel as more experienced than herself professionally, visited Mabel and Elsie at Grove Farm a number of times over the next few years, and wrote Mabel regularly from Honolulu. Often her subject was the operation of the health centers, and the experience of nursing within the Board of Health's complex organization. In one letter she told Mabel, "You have done mighty well to keep up all those centers, for during November your clinics had the largest enrollment and case attendance it has ever had." She added, "Your being Field Supervisor will help so much in getting Public Health nurses and nursing on a much higher plane."[16]

Still, the continuing political problems with the Board of Health concerned them both. They were worried about nursing staff retention problems and the lack of a policy for public health nursing salary ranges. They knew that Palama Settlement had a salary scale for its nurses, and Smyth observed that on all islands, "Eleven nurses resigned during the year [1928–1929]. ... This tremendous turnover in the nursing staff is certainly most detrimental to efficient service to the public." [17]

There was only one set salary schedule for all nurses employed in the Territorial Board of Health, whether she was a graduate or non-graduate public health nurse. Smyth observed:

> There is absolutely no inducement to the ambitious and worthwhile public health nurse, and she is the only type we want, to remain after she has seen the island. In order that the territory may have a more stable and permanent staff of nurses, it is recommended that a sliding scale of salaries be initiated.[18]

In addition, demands upon the rural public health nurses on every island were increasing. The Big Island field supervisor of nursing Jane Service, R.N., summed it up for her colleagues stating she felt like a "[v]oice crying in the wilderness."

> I have so many *different* things to do that while trying to do one I always feel the pull of something else. While in the office catching up on record work, (do we hear a sardonic Ha-ha?), I feel a sense of guilt when I think of the many people, human beings, I ought to be helping outside. When outside I am burdened with a sense of delinquency toward my records. If I could do *only* Tuberculosis, *only* Maternity and Infancy, or, as in most cases, if I could only devote all my time to school work."

Nurses continued to work hard at the clinics, however, and Smyth wrote in 1930, "Greater and continued efforts are constantly being made to interest the Hawaiian mothers in the baby conferences."[19] Kauai's infant mortality rate continued to decrease, dropping to 74.97 per 1000 by 1932, and Margaret Bergen wrote to Mabel, "Kauai is getting more and more to be a finished picture as you get your brush going. We are already using it as Exhibit A."[20]

Mabel had changed her mind about leaving her Territorial nursing position after Appleton's dismissal for at least two reasons. The first was the appointment of Smyth, whom she greatly respected as a nurse. The other seems to have been Mabel's awareness that, behind the scenes in Honolulu, individuals realized that the Board of Health administration had underestimated the public health needs of the community prompted by Hawaii's "baby boom" and resulting demographic change. Hiscock's professional survey from a national public health care perspective gave the board and its staff a new focus.[21]

Her decade in administration gave Mabel practical experience in the problems of administrative leadership, professional rivalry, and the role of voluntary community organizations. This was thorough preparation for her next assignment: working with her sister Elsie shaping the relationship of plantation health care and clinical medicine in the form of Kauai's general hospital.

PART III 1931–1959

Chapter Eleven

FROM DREAM TO REALITY

Mabel was prepared by 1930 to act on several of Professor Hiscock's recommendations and to apply them to health care on Kauai. As supervisor of the new generalized nursing system, she was able to bring about closer coordination in the work of tuberculosis, maternal and infant health, and school and social service nurses.

Tuberculosis, as Smyth had reported, continued to require the heaviest Territorial attention, and Mabel Wilcox's nurses spent at least half of their time with tuberculosis uncertainties. The care of children who had contact with known consumption cases, or who were seriously underweight, were more and more a public health problem. At Mahelona hospital the staff initiated summer "health camps" on the sanatorium's grounds for children with pre-tuberculosis signs, chosen by public health nurses for eight to ten weeks of controlled diet and exercise.[1]

Hiscock had recommended the development of facilities for children noting that a preventorium, as it was called, had been built on Maui, and Mabel began to campaign for one on Kauai in 1929. She turned to G. N. for capital funds. The County preventorium at Mahelona, with dormitory space for 50 children, was built after her uncle donated $34,000 for its construction. In April 1931 G. N. wrote, "The preventorium [is] to be a gift from me to the people of Kauai." It was named "Kaiakea" for the eighteenth-century Kauai chief whose kindness for people had been so remarkable that he was given the name meaning "the boundless sea."[2] It was estimated that more than 300 children on Kauai were actively exposed to tuberculosis in their homes and were likely to become victims of the disease.

Ethel Damon noted that when G. N. was informed that the building might have to be made smaller he replied, "Kaiakea, don't you think that's a good name for it ... I told [the hospital] to get whatever they needed. Those children need it. Why, I'd sell my last shirt to get that building up." Of all of G. N.'s many philanthropic causes, one of his keenest interests was the care of children and youth. He and Mabel worked closely on the plans for Kaiakea during the last few years of his life. While some tuberculosis authorities began to switch attention from preventoria to expanded school health class programs later in the 30s, Kaiakea functioned to increase children's resistance to tuberculosis to a point where they could again lead safe and normal lives.[3]

Annual operating support for the preventorium at Mahelona came from County and Territorial funds, and these were supplemented by the Kauai Tuberculosis Association, which Mabel organized in 1929. Funds were raised from the yearly sale of 50,000 penny Christmas seals (distributed by the national association) and donations from businesses and individuals. Mabel was one of the directors of the

Sheet of 1929 TB Christmas Seal's was the first entry in an album kept by Mabel as Secretary of Kauai Tuberculosis Association. Seal is on the right.

Kauai Tuberculosis Association for the next 20 years, working with Bernice E. L. Hundley and others. She reported that the 1935 sales were 14 cents per capita "which is one of the largest percentages in the United States and is the largest in Hawaii."

She found ways to supplement public support for health care with private donations from the community such as the Mokihana Club. For example, Mahelona Hospital, with support from the Association, was able to increase its early diagnosis campaign for tuberculin skin test in all Kauai

Mabel Wilcox. c. 1930

schools—6,300 children—making the island the first district outside Honolulu to implement such a project. The Association also furnished free X-ray films for a number of tests. Its largest contribution, however, was the funding for two more public health nurses on Mabel's Territorial staff who did intensive case finding and follow-up with patients and families. It was hoped that the Territory would find support for the two positions as soon as government funds were appropriated. One of these nursing positions was taken over after five years, but the other was continued by the Association until 1940. Mabel believed that the ultimate

Richard K.C. Lee and Ira Hiscock at Yale University in 1965. Hiscock continued his Hawaii associations. Richard Lee had been Hiscock's graduate student in the 1930's and became director of the Territorial Department of Health.

achievement of the organization was that it helped people overcome their fears of tuberculosis.[4]

Hiscock returned to the Islands in 1935 to update his health survey. He was invited to visit Kauai by the Kauai Chamber of Commerce, Mabel Wilcox, V. A. Harl, M.D., of Kilauea Sugar Company, and pathologist A. M. Ecklund, M.D. Hiscock's brief study of public health work on Kauai covered such topics as communicable diseases, laboratory services, maternity and child hygiene, public health nursing, and sanitation. He noted "the Tuberculosis Association was a valuable voluntary health agency in the development of an active tuberculosis program in the Island devoted to public health nursing, assistance with school surveys, and health education." Hiscock also noted the cooperation of the seven Territorial public health nurses and four nurses from plantations, adding "the Tuberculosis association has for some years assisted in the provision of field nursing service—in addition to a nurse provided by the Board of Child Welfare."[5]

At the same time that Mabel was involved in expanding public health nursing, she was beginning to plan a new hospital with her uncle, sister and Dora Isenberg. The old Lihue Hospital had taken care of the workers and families of Lihue Plantation, Grove Farm, and Kipu Ranch for nearly 40 years; its medical services were both a contractual perquisite of the plantations, along with housing, and a cost of doing business.

Plantation medicine, also known as industrial medicine, provided the underpinning of institutional care in rural Hawaii until the 1960s. During the long period when plantations continued to have a commanding influence on the economic and social life of Kauai, plantation medical services were provided by company physicians, nurses, and *kokua*, or assistants, working out of small hospitals and dispensaries.

As Ethel Damon wrote in *Koamalu*, her history of the Rice and Isenberg families, "The initial building with equipment for some thirty patients was the gift of the owners in the plantations of Lihue, Kipu, and Grove Farm. Over one hundred cases were treated during the first year, one-third of these being typhoid, one sixth for beriberi." Facilities in the 45-bed Lihue Hospital had been improved when needed. Between 1907 and 1919 a new operating room, X-ray equipment, a children's ward, and a separate tuberculosis ward called the "Sun House" were added.[6] The isolated tuberculosis ward accommodated five or six infected patients, though it went out of use with the opening of Mahelona Hospital. Another small structure called the "Old Men's Home" later was built for the long-term care of retired plantation single men. The hospital superintendent's family lived next door in a house provided by the hospital, and the nurses, the cook and laundress's families also lived on hospital grounds.

Lihue Hospital's superintendent for many years was J. M. Kuhns, M.D., the doctor who had been in charge at Kealia plantation hospital and Mahelona before coming to Lihue Plantation Company in 1921. Like other plantation doctors, Kuhns was expected to care for surgery, dermatology, internal medicine, obstetrics, pediatrics, and other cases. In 1929 Nils Larsen, M.D., the medical director of The Queen's Hospital, spent several days visiting Kuhns in Lihue and his assistant, William D. Balfour, M.D., at Kealia, which was part of the enlarged Lihue Plantation. Larsen published what he called a "field portrait of Kuhns' practice" for his colleagues at Queen's in Honolulu, the first of many articles Larsen wrote about plantation medicine in Hawaii.

Larsen observed Kuhns' treatment of varied cases: "A crushed hand, a gunshot wound of the foot, an appendix, a bad heart, chronic constipation, a sarcoma, a caesarian, high blood pressure, a meningitis in serum therapy—anything that a doctor might meet, all well taken care of ." He went out with Kuhns late at night to visit a case in the field:

> We were going to bed one night about 11 when the telephone rang. A patient with pneumonia, some seven miles away, was worried and was afraid to face the night. The doctor dressed and went out to a small Hawaiian house on the shore. The man with pneumonia just needed some encouragement. He got it. We returned about midnight, at 7:30 I met the doctor for breakfast, he had been out again at 2 a.m. but was already to meet another day. For a month he had not averaged over four hours of sleep per night.[7]

Larsen asked,

> Is it possible to properly care for so many people? A great deal of time could not be spent with each, but with a proficient nurse or two and a trained native helper who took care of most of the minor injuries, dressings, etc., it was so organized that the doctor really had a clean efficient hospital. He had time for two or three major operations a week, time to make daily rounds, time to visit patients, time for 12 baby clinics during the week, and some time left for his family.

Marvin Brennecke, M.D., was recruited by Kuhns in 1931 from Washington University in St. Louis, Kuhns' alma mater. He looked back on his mentor's practice of medicine this way: "I worked with him for about a year and a half, I learned a great deal from him. He was an excellent doctor and we of course worked well together. I was paid a hundred dollars a month and maintenance, but I got about ten thousand dollars salary in experiences each month. It was just fantastic." Kuhns and Brennecke's everyday routine included early morning work in the Lihue dispensary from nine to eleven, then to the plantation's dispensary in Hanamaulu from eleven to twelve. If they had other surgery, they would do it after lunch.[8]

Kuhns said half-jokingly that there were two required skills for a plantation doctor at the Lihue Hospital: perform an appendectomy and dispense medicines. There were nine brown bottles—very large bottles numbered one through nine and they were kept on a shelf. Kuhns remembered that whenever he finished seeing a patient he would shout out something like "Number 1 … Number 9" and the quantity of pills to dispense. The pills would be put in a paper bag and handed to the patient.

The other personnel of Lihue Hospital included a head plantation nurse and two other registered nurses, a head orderly, two other orderlies, a cook and cook's helper, two laundresses and several maids. Typical of most plantations was the dispensary assistant's position. At Lihue for many years, Masao "Togo" Kashiwahara helped Kuhns. Called "Dr. Togo" by patients, the medical education Kashiwahara received was from Kuhns and later from Sam Wallis, M.D. Brennecke recalled that Togo would see patients and "could make a diagnosis, and then he'd call Dr. Kuhns or myself and we would care for [the patient]." A Lihue nurse, Kay Irwin recalled,

> Togo was a very smart man. I think he was only about 17 when he came, something like that, but he was very smart and his potential was soon recognized. He soon became the supervisor. Dr. Wallis once said that if he couldn't do an appendectomy, maybe Togo could do it because he had that much confidence in Togo's ability. Togo was good at minor repair work. That kind of thing would be frowned on, [now] not even tolerated, but this was back in the days of the Territory and he was as good as anybody.[9]

According to his co-workers at the hospital and dispensary, Togo played a significant role, from filling Kuhns' prescriptions and operating hospital X-ray equipment to picking up the mail for the hospital and milk for the patients.

The staff was kept busy with approximately 1,700 dispensary calls per month, or between 50–60 employees a day, from Lihue Plantation, Grove Farm, and Kipu, as well as from private patients as there was no other dispensary in the Lihue area. At the hospital there were approximately 750 days a month reported for the use of hospital beds—a figure that would undoubtedly have been larger if Kuhns had used the hospital for confinements. But in the years before a new hospital maternity ward was available, infections were feared. Brennecke recalled:

> Over here Dr. Kuhns delivered all of his pregnancies, all of the mothers, at home. He would never have a delivery at the hospital.

That originated from the work of Ignaz Semmelweiss in Austria where they found that the mortality from deliveries was greater in hospitals. Dr. Kuhns was of that school of thought, and it had been so ingrained in the medical profession that the hospitals were the worst place to be when you had a baby, because this caused infection. For that reason, Dr. Kuhns delivered them all at home. He and his nurse could go out at nine o'clock, they would go out and deliver baby, two o'clock in the morning. ... I don't know how Dr. Kuhns did it, but he did it very well.[10]

Kuhns estimated that he had delivered 4,000 mothers, or an average of two or three a week, in 44 years as a general practitioner.

One troubling weakness of Lihue Hospital, however, was the growing number of non-plantation patients. As early as 1919 G. N. Wilcox and the other hospital directors had noted:

> There is no other place for the sick to turn, and while this Hospital is maintained and conducted mainly to serve the plantations of this locality, there is a large and constantly growing number of people here (attracted by the plantations) who are not so employed.

In 1930 Lihue Hospital reported that 20 percent of care was for non-plantation people, many of them indigent cases. The opening of new County and Territorial offices in Lihue, and the expansion of commercial activity that increased the town's governmental and economic importance drew more people to the hospital,[11] as did construction of the island's first deepwater harbor in Lihue. G. N. Wilcox bought the entire issue of local bonds for construction to avoid delays from a public sale, and he personally oversaw the engineering until the breakwater was completed in 1930. G. N. Wilcox's final years were well remembered because of his connection with the project. It was time to plan and build a new hospital which could meet the needs of the entire community, plantation and non-plantation alike. Although Wilcox did not live to see his dream become a reality, the new hospital was built with funds from the G. N. Wilcox Trust, and it was dedicated to him as a memorial. Mabel was the catalyst.

Another reason for the building of the new hospital had to do with plantation reform and the changing needs of Hawaii's labor force. Sugar plantations in Hawaii had experienced strikes and labor turnover, and the industry's membership organization—the Hawaiian Sugar Planters' Association (HSPA)—established an Industrial Service Bureau in 1920 to reform policies for laborers' housing and medical benefits. The HSPA retained the mainland industrial relations firm of

Curtis, Fosdick, and Belknap to assess policies in 1925, and its study reached several conclusions that led the way to reforms. One of these changes was the hiring of The Queen's Hospital's Larsen as its advisor in 1930. Larsen became for industrial medicine in Hawaii what Yale University's Ira Hiscock was for public health in the Territory, and both men were committed to preventive medicine and health education. Like Mabel and others in public health reforms in Hawaii, they tried to further coalescence of preventive and curative medicine at the time when clinical medicine and public health on the mainland were beginning to follow separate strategies.[12]

The Curtis, Fosdick, and Belknap study found that the most serious problem of plantation medical service was that it was not standardized. The report concluded that "The open violation of the labor contract guaranteeing free medical service, refusals to attend the sick, the reluctance to attend confinement cases, the charging of fees out of all proportion to the workers' ability to pay, inadequate supervision of the work of plantation or welfare nurses, case diagnosis and dispensation of drugs by nurses, and other questionable practices in the administration of medical services have resulted in severe censure and criticism of physicians on some plantations by medical colleagues and health officials.[13]

The report observed "the private practice of plantation physicians has been the cause of considerable criticism by reason of the attention given it in detriment to plantation service and the fees charged which, in many quarters, are considered excessive." Larsen agreed with these assessments, and some years later he wrote:

> Hospitals that 'just ran' were not giving their patients up-to-date and proper service. The results, as you know, of lack of service are not so much added deaths as they are unnecessary operations, overly long periods in the hospital, wrong diagnoses and therefore unnecessary suffering, wrong use of equipment, and wasteful methods because they were unchecked, and with this an unconscious, uncritical attitude developing on the part of nurses and doctors.[14]

Larsen believed that "the time of the 'lone wolf' in medicine has disappeared with the doctor's buggy. No one, with the complexity of diagnosis and treatment today, can possibly carry all the details for all cases in his head, or quickly find it in his books."

When Robert Worth, M.D. looked back on his experience with plantation medicine when he was Kauai District Health Officer he observed.

"Company medicine as a system was a forerunner of an HMO. That basically was an HMO model before the name was invented and it was vulnerable to several problems: One was you're locked in on a patient so that if you have a personality clash you've had it. This is from the patient's point of view.

A few of them had a chip on their shoulder."[15]

Worth added, "There were no gaps in terms of accessibility to plantation care. The plantation environment meant that there was really a GP close by almost every plantation." But Worth drew attention to deficiencies in the quality of plantation medicine:

I think one difficulty had to do with an ego problem that developed among doctors who were part of a Feudal Society. You know they gave advice—the patients didn't ever question their opinion—no one ever challenged them—they seldom were confronted with a doctor who knew more than they did about anything.

I think in a rural environment, where doctors are quite isolated and there are no other doctors around, or, very few, and they're almost all general practitioners—they seldom refer patients so they don't have the practice of being humble.[16]

Although some of the plantation doctors used the local public health/district health nurse very well, but some of them had a chip on their shoulder. If the public health nurse referred somebody in who wasn't on the verge of death, they got fussy about it. They didn't want to be bothered. They thought it was an inappropriate referral.[17]

Worth was describing the medical world on Kauai's plantation that Mabel and her nurses knew intimately. Despite the exemplary work of physicians like Kuhns, professional health care on the plantations was uneven. It was Larsen in the 1930s who brought the perspective of hospital standardization and the American College of Surgeons to his work with the plantations in Hawaii. As medical historian Rosemary Stevens notes, the standardization system was designed for several purposes: to certify the small hospital as a well-equipped local surgical and obstetrical center; and "to prod the medical staff in local hospitals to police avaricious and inappropriate behavior by the hospital's surgeons." Larsen welcomed Malcolm MacEachern, M.D., Superintendent of the Vancouver General Hospital and Director of the American College of Physicians and Surgeons, to Honolulu in 1936 to discuss standardization. It was the subject of Larsen's editorial in the second issue of *Plantation*

Health Bulletin, the new quarterly publication published by the HSPA for the staff of all plantations. The bulletin was intended to improve medical service by sharing articles written by plantation physicians and disseminating knowledge of the results of experimental nutritional work in preventive medicine underway at the Ewa Plantation health Project and the Research Department of The Queen's Hospital.[18]

Mabel was active in these hospital reforms. She undertook a survey, at G. N.'s behest, of the existing plantation facilities for acute care and outpatient services at Eleele, Kealia, Kilauea, Koloa, Lihue, Makaweli, and Waimea plantations. Larsen and Hiscock provided Mabel with the requirements for hospital standardization from the American College of Surgeons and with guidelines for health centers from the American Public Health Association.

Elizabeth Middleton who later administered the G. N. Wilcox Memorial Hospital said, "Miss Mabel wanted a hospital that people could go to for proper care. She felt they weren't properly taken care of in plantation hospitals." As part of improvements in plantation medicine, Mabel led the organization of the Kauai Nurses Association in 1932, which brought together registered nurses on the island from plantation hospitals, Mahelona, and public health work following the organization of the Nurses Associates of the Territory of Hawaii. In monthly educational and social meetings the nurses discussed the developments in the medical and nursing field. Larsen, Smyth, and Dora Isenberg were among the early guest speakers. In references to these meetings Mabel later said, "Without these programs interest would have lagged." There were 34 charter members of the Kauai Nurses Association, and they elected Mabel president and reelected her annually until 1946.[19]

In 1931 Mabel had been able to take a leave from Territorial nursing to take four summer graduate courses in public health nursing, health education, rural government, and rural communities in the School of Applied Sciences at Western Reserve University in Cleveland, Ohio, which helped her prepare a written proposal for the organization of the administration and staffing of a new Lihue Hospital.

Mabel proposed that the hospital would be an "open staff," in other words, independent, medical institution.[20] The intent of the hospital proposal, probably written before her uncle's death in 1933, was to make the new hospital more than a plantation facility by providing hospital admitting privileges for qualified non-plantation doctors. Such a plan, Mabel said, would "allow other Doctors now practicing locally to care for their patients in the hospital." As Richard K. C. Lee, M.D., the Territorial deputy health officer at the time, later observed, "The Lihue Hospital in those days was a plantation hospital and doctors who came home to practice who were not part of the plantation couldn't use the hospital."[21] Mabel "always looked ahead," Lee said, and she was thinking particularly of the licensed physicians to whom the plantation hospitals were closed for their use.

Mabel enumerated functions of the hospital's doctors. Her list included: attending plantation cases in the field and in the hospital; conducting dispensaries, prenatal conferences, child health conferences, cooperating with chest clinics, and other diagnostic services; and holding at least weekly meetings with the resident and attending physicians for discussion and analysis of cases. She added that the plantation doctor "may have the privilege of attending private cases, but at all times his foremost concern should be the matter of preventive medicine for the plantations who employ him."[22]

Mabel addressed hospital nursing services in a way that was consistent with the reform concept of the hospital as a health center. She proposed that a field nurse be employed to work in cooperation with the Lihue Board of Health nurse under direction of the Kauai Field Supervisor, as had been done by the Kauai Tuberculosis Association and the Board of Child Welfare with their nurses. Mabel's thinking about cooperative health work and recommendations for the interrelations of the hospital, clinics, and public health nursing were influenced by *Community Health Organization:* a manual edited by Hiscock and published by the philanthropic Commonwealth Fund based in New York. The guide evolved from the American Public Health Association's Committee on administrative practice and Hiscock's extensive involvement in the local, state, and national agencies. Mabel marked the passages in Hiscock's book relating to hospitals, outpatient facilities, and forms of cooperation.

Before the Second World War, Kauai might have seemed a tight little island controlled by the sugar plantations who built and operated their own small hospitals and dispensaries, and employed their own physicians, nurses, and other staff. However, in response to professional standards nationally and the needs of the growing number on non-plantation private patients, Mabel wanted Lihue Hospital to acquire improved equipment and facilities. She also wanted to give medical practitioners new opportunities on Kauai. As such, she started to work full time in 1935 on specific plans for the new hospital, and her efforts gained increasing support.

Unfortunately, her Uncle George would not be there to see his niece carry out what he had started. In 1933, G. N. Wilcox died. G. N.'s death brought Gaylord, Elsie, and Mabel together in what today would be called a "management team." Gaylord, or G. P. as he was called, left his position with American Factors in Honolulu to be president of Grove Farm. As Grove Farm Company officers the siblings shared the approval of new building programs and technological improvements for the plantation.

Gaylord also took responsibility for negotiating the economic interests of Grove Farm and Lihue Plantation in the new fees the hospital would charge the plantations for the acute care of their employees and families. He and Dora Isenberg used their executive influence at American Factors, the owner of Lihue Plantation, to convey a 15-acre site for the hospital.

Elsie continued the family's tradition of charity giving by making many personal gifts and serving as a member of the beneficiary committee of the G. N. Wilcox Trust. It was Elsie who sought advice on the architectural design of the new hospital main building from her long-time family friend and well-established Honolulu architect, Charles W. Dickey.[23] Elsie's own progressive vision of the modern hospital pictured it as the controlling center for Kauai's health care system—an idea she soon learned was not entirely shared by all of Kauai's plantation managers and plantation physicians. She also saw the general hospital as a way for second generation Japanese and Filipinos to adopt American ways.

Mabel complemented her brother's and sister's hospital interest by clarifying the standards of the facilities and staff needed by the hospital. She provided a liaison to the Queen's Hospital in Honolulu by setting up operating procedures, and recruiting and selecting the first hospital superintendent, as recommended by Queen's. The three of them saw the hospital as making G. N.'s dream come true and their leadership gave significant coherence to the institutional framework of Kauai in the coming years.

Chapter Twelve

RETIREMENT FROM
TERRITORIAL NURSING

Mabel's father died in 1929 and when her mother died five years later —a year after G. N. —Mabel and Elsie started to make the Grove Farm house more of their own home. Grove Farm's architecture lent itself to their public, professional, and private lives. Elsie kept her father's office as her office when she was not away in Honolulu at Territorial Senate sessions, with a separate, small desk for a secretary. Across the hall, Mabel adapted her parents' bedroom for her own office when Emma had to be moved into their sitting room during her last illness. After her mother's death, Mabel continued to use the office for her own personal papers, investment and banking correspondence, and later, copies of board of trustees records and plans for the new hospital.

While Board of Health nurses used the new County Building Annex in Lihue for their office after 1930, Mabel kept busy in the cottage behind the house with the Kauai Tuberculosis Association and the newly formed Kauai Nurse's Association.

With the older generation gone, Elsie and Mabel continued to preserve their privacy and their personal identification at Grove Farm, especially after the death of their sister Etta. They continued to enjoy Etta's and Digby's children. Dorthea Sloggett had been married to Harrison Rice Cooke in 1931 at Grove Farm while her mother, grandmother, and G. N. were still alive. It was reported "the house was beautifully decorated with large bouquets of white gladiola and mixed flowers of various shades. The fireplace before which the ceremony took place was banked with ferns and sprays orchids." Several other weddings elsewhere kept their minds off the recent family deaths.

Mabel and Elsie celebrated the marriage of their late brother Charles'
son Sam to Edith King in Honolulu in 1934 and one of Charles'
daughter, Lois, two years later to Frederick Klebahn. Gaylord's son,
Albert, was also married, to Louise Shingle in 1937 at Puhi.[1]

After Uncle George's death, they closed G. N.'s cottage but
preserved all his furnishings, a testament to their beloved uncle.
The old plantation office continued to be used for the Grove Farm
company directors' meetings, even after a larger modern plantation
office was built in Puhi following G. N.'s death. Elsie and Mabel
made changes to parts of Grove Farm, however, combining a sense
of their missionary past and an artistic present. The style reflected
their domestic tastes, and decorative arts writers of the period called
it "Modern Colonial." They covered over flowered wallpaper designs
in the downstairs rooms with plasterboard and painted them in pale
colors as a simpler background for their arts and crafts and Colonial
Revival furniture. The Wilcoxes had always taken a special interest in
the cabinetwork and designs of the Hilo Boarding School manual arts
training program. Emma's brother, Levi Lyman, was president of the
boarding school and his wife Nettie oversaw the woodcrafts shop and
sale of furniture made of *koa*. They were reproductions or adaptations
of nineteenth-century American chairs, tables, and beds and were put
into everyday use throughout the house and guest cottage.

Built-in bookshelves and cabinets were designed by the architect
Hart Wood for two rooms at the end of the house where Emma's cabinet
of curiosities was preserved. Elsie and Mabel tracked down Emma's
piano, which had been sold, and repurchased it. The many Hawaiian
artifacts their father and uncle had collected were moved from G. N.'s
cluttered "bachelor" sleeping quarters and old plantation office into
the refurbished end rooms, along with their growing collection of
historical books, including Hawaiian language imprints.

By 1930 the Grove Farm house contained the works of such artists
as Otto Wix, Juliette May Fraser, D. Howard Hitchcock, A. R. Gurrey,
and Charles W. Bartlett. Bartlett had been chosen to paint a double
portrait of Sam and Emma in 1929, showing them sitting on the front
lanai. David Forbes, the art historian, considers it one of Bartlett's finest
paintings. Elsie continued to add paintings, watercolors, prints and
pastel drawings by Bartlett. Elsie, Mabel, and Ethel Damon had become
good friends of Bartlett and his wife and some of the works were gifts.
As part of their family's personal memories of Waioli Mission House,
Elsie and Mabel asked Bartlett in 1937 to paint a landscape of Waioli
that they could hang in the Grove Farm house one hundred years

after Waioli Mission House was built. Bartlett's impressionist painting reached out in the familiar silvery light of the Waioli valley into the borderland between imagination, memory, and reality. It captured Elsie and Mabel's aesthetic taste in landscapes.

Mabel and Elsie planned the Waioli Mission centennial celebration, to take place in 1934. About one thousand people came to Hanalei and celebrated the founding of the mission church. The Rev. Alfred Akiona preached in Hawaiian on the text in Genesis—"This Bethel is indeed the house of God"—and seven Hawaiian choirs from Kauai churches gathered. At the well-attended afternoon reception in front of the preserved Mission House, it was noted that Waioli "was a picture of color and an exhibition of informal, spontaneous social fellowship and song which carried everything with it." The singing was impressive: the members of the choirs presented "Hawaii Aloha" and "Na Molokama."[2]

In addition to Waioli, Elsie gave direction to the G. N. Wilcox Trust in support of many projects. The foundation funded the Kauai YMCA's assembly and recreation hall at Camp Naue in Haena in 1934 as a memorial to G. N. The Trust also donated capital funds for construction of a new boy's dormitory at Punahou School, dedicated in 1937, but it was the foundation's announcement of a $200,000 gift, its largest, that helped make the new hospital in Lihue possible.[3]

Mabel anticipated the extent and importance of the planning needed for the new hospital when she retired from her Territorial position in 1934 as Field Supervisor of Nursing for Kauai. Several years later Ira Hiscock drew attention to the changes in health care in Hawaii in an article published in the *American Journal of Public Health*, titled "Health Work on a Sugar Plantation in Hawaii." Hiscock's conclusions applied well to achievements of Mabel's 20 years of nursing on Kauai. "The Territorial Board of Health staff cooperates in the public health work on the plantation," he wrote, "and provides nursing, baby conferences, tuberculosis clinics, and inspection service for the outside area." Hiscock described the notable reduction of preventable diseases among the population of Hawaii in these measurable terms: [4]

> Through the activities of the Territorial Board of Health, with the cooperation of many official and voluntary agencies, smallpox had become a medical curiosity; typhoid and tuberculosis have been greatly reduced; and diphtheria is well on the way to control. Over 60 percent of the preschool children have been given prophylactic injections against diphtheria in this Territory of some 400,000

people, and there was not a death from this disease during the fiscal year 1934–1935. The tuberculosis death rate has dropped from over 200 in 1920 to an annual average of under 100 for the past 5 years. The infant mortality rate in the Territory was 65 for fiscal year 1935, with an annual average rate of 82 for the previous 5 years.

In June 1935, Mabel Smyth wrote a tribute to Mabel in *The Pacific Coast Journal of Nursing*. Looking back on Mabel's career in nursing, she concluded with this assessment:

> With clarity of purpose and wisdom in leadership Miss Wilcox has developed an unusual spirit of loyalty and devotion among her corps of nurses and superiors. This is not limited, however, to her own immediate group, for every nurse, as well as public school teacher and principal on the island, turns to her for inspiration and leadership in matters pertaining to individual and community well-being.[5]

After retirement, Mabel took a long relaxing vacation. Accompanied by her old colleague and friend, Margaret Bergen, who also was retiring from years of social service, Mabel took a sixteen-week cruise to the South Pacific, Australia, New Zealand, India, East Africa, and South America. Lorin Tarr Gill, of the *Honolulu Star-Bulletin*, interviewed Mabel just before she departed. "If you really want to write anything about me, and I really don't see why you should," she told Gill, "don't you think you should wait until after I go?" Gill reported that Mabel's question was asked in all seriousness and "those who know her will understand."[6] Like G. N., Mabel was reserved in public and avoided publicity about her life.

Mabel and Bergen sailed aboard the British Cunard White Star liner "Franconia." Mabel wrote home during her voyage, posting her mail at various ports. In her first letter she wrote:

> Our routine so far is to "lean on the button twice" (so designated by the stewardess) sometime after 7 a.m. and she brings us orange juice, coffee, and melba toast. ... So far I've slept most of the afternoon but am about slept out now.

In the first days they finished off the food sent with them from Grove Farm and by other friends in Honolulu: guava jelly, poha jam, nuts, avocados, papayas, dried fish, and about a gallon of poi. "There is no danger of our starving or losing weight," Mabel wrote. Later, she wrote to her cousin Helen Lockett Lyman at Grove Farm:

I don't know anything quite so good that has happened on the trip as getting mail at Auckland! It has seemed such a long time since we had any word from home. Time hasn't dragged, but it just seemed good to get news of you all. ... I sort of wish I were there & we were off to Hanalei!

When Mabel returned to Kauai a few months later, her planning for the new hospital continued in consultation with Jay Kuhns and W. D. Balfour of Lihue Plantation. In September 1935 the doctors reported that the hospital should require 100 beds to meet the needs of Lihue and Kealia. They proposed divisions into surgical, medical, children's, isolation and obstetrical wards, with a nursery and two operating rooms. They suggested "a two story building, to be built in such form that additions can easily be made. Good equipment is absolutely essential and should be taken into consideration when the cost of the building is figured."[7]

Nils Larsen meanwhile advised Mabel on rules, regulations, methods of staff appointments and salary scales. He wrote her in September 1935:

As to increased cost in developing a standardized hospital, it undoubtedly would cost more in actual money, but I believe by having the necessary equipment and organization, you would keep the hospital more full than if you run it without necessary equipment and in this way it should pay for itself. At the Queen's, in spite of all the objections made each time we have added a new department or new equipment—and the usual objection would be that we cannot afford—we have constantly increased our income, more or less parallel with our increased cost of overhead.[8]

Larsen added, "I find I did not compliment you on your vision in developing this unit, but I really feel nothing would be more helpful in raising the standard of service to the sick on the Island of Kauai." He made suggestions about hospital architecture:

May I caution you in the development of your plans to avoid the usual break of allowing an architect to draw plans without any knowledge of the difficulty of organization and hospital control. By arranging wards and rooms in certain ways, many times it is possible to cut down on the number of nurses needed, especially in watching patients at night.

Another mistake made on some of the hospital plans locally, has been to accept mainland ideas, whereas in this climate we can make use of full sliding doors and windows and greater lanai space than they ever think of using on the mainland. I feel our hospital building should definitely take into consideration our local climate in regard to direction of trade winds etc.

The new voluntary hospital was incorporated as a not-for-profit corporation governed by nine trustees, and they first met in March 1936 in the old Grove Farm office. Besides Mabel, Elsie, and G. P., the other charter trustees were Dora Isenberg, the senior member and the only remaining link to the other founders of the Lihue Hospital in 1898; Caleb Burns, manager of Lihue Plantation; E. H. W. Broadbent, manager of Grove Farm; Alan Faye, architect and manager of his family's Waimea Sugar Company; Philip Rice, attorney; and Archibald Ecklund, M.D., who represented the Kauai Medical Society.[9]

Not all of the Kauai plantation managers and doctors were ready to use the services of the proposed new hospital. As Elizabeth Middleton, R.N., put it later, "opinions differed" and were divided along island geographical lines. Doctors, especially from west side plantations, felt their small hospital and dispensaries had developed a high standard of health care. Alan Faye's brother Lindsay, manager of Kekaha Sugar Company, was responsible for the 35-bed hospital built in Waimea in 1929. He wrote Elsie about the plans for G. N. Wilcox Memorial Hospital: [10]

> The only objection to such an institution, to my mind, would be that it might attract too many independent doctors, thus flooding the market and making the profession less attractive to good men. This might be especially true with plantation doctors who usually have good outside practice besides their regular plantation work.

Kekaha's plantation physician, Burt Wade, M.D., was more outspoken. He was critical of Elsie Wilcox and much later said, "There was a move on the island to centralize everything in Lihue and shut down all the local hospitals on the outside."[11]

On the other hand, Larsen gave the plan for the "open staff" hospital in Lihue his full support. In spite of his active affiliation with the Hawaii Sugar Planters Association, he expected the new hospital would be more than a plantation hospital.

The trustees sought advice on building plans from the well-established Honolulu architect, Charles W. Dickey, who was also a long-time Wilcox family friend. Dickey responded with a two story hipped-roof plan featuring *lanais* and deep roof overhangs to shade large windows and provide ample ventilation, as Larsen had suggested. Dickey had worked on other island hospital projects: recently he had

Architect's rendering of plans for the G. N. Wilcox Memorial Hospital in Lihue designed by Charles W. Dickey in 1937.

designed the Waialua Plantation Hospital on Oahu, Puunene Hospital on Maui, and Kula Sanatorium on the Big Island. Dickey completed drawings for the two-story building in 1937 and the job was awarded to the Honolulu contractor, Ralph Woolley.[12] One is reminded of what historian Rosemary Stevens has written about voluntary American hospital design in the 1930s: "Hospitals were also important examples of the clean, functional lines of modern technology and modern architecture. Numerous new (expensive) buildings spoke of simplicity, sunshine, sanitation, science, rationality, modernism and common sense." Mabel intended that the hospital be a modern example of efficiency, hygiene, and safety and improved clinical standards.

The physical layout of the fireproof, steel-reinforced concrete building had five six-person wards for men on the first floor and five additional wards on the second floor for women. These rooms represented a shift to smaller wards where more privacy was valued; each patient's bed was curtained off for examinations, and there was a room between each ward with a toilet, bath, and shower. The hospital also had semi-private rooms and nine expensive single rooms with private bathrooms and lanais. Dickey originally proposed floor plans and elevations of a separate outpatient dispensary to replace the old Lihue Hospital and a Nurses' Home, but the trustees changed their minds, probably because of estimated costs of construction. Consequently Lihue Plantation was asked by the Trustees to build a new dispensary next to the hospital, and Grove Farm to build the Nurses' Home. In reality, Lihue Plantation put off building the new outpatient dispensary indefinitely, with Lihue Plantation and Grove Farm continuing to use the old hospital building as a dispensary and

Sam Wallis remaining in charge. But, G. P. Wilcox, who had launched a program to centralize Grove Farm plantation operations at Puhi after G. N. Wilcox's death, asked Alan Faye, with the help of Honolulu architect Thomas Perkins and Mabel, to design the nurses' residence. It consisted of 20 modern individual apartments, a dining room, and living room built around four landscaped courtyards. Grove Farm built the Nurses' Home so that it could be occupied when the hospital opened for its first patient in November 1938.[13]

G. N. Wilcox Memorial Hospital Nurses' Home built around four courts, 1938-1939. Deigned by Thomas Perkins and constructed by Grove Farm Company.

Nurses' Home living room and dining room (beyond).

Upon the recommendation of Larsen, Mabel and the trustees in November 1937 asked Anna Grace Williams, R.N., Director of Education at Queen's to take the position of Hospital Superintendent and Director of Nursing. Williams accepted and began to organize the recruitment of staff and orders for equipment, while living and working out of the Grove Farm house for some months during construction of the hospital. Nearing completion of the hospital during the summer of 1938, Grove Farm was a beehive of activity. Hanna Hotvedt, the dietician selected after her internship in clinical dietetics at Cook County Hospital in Chicago, was also put up at Grove Farm. She recalled that "we were treated as family members," and was fascinated to be introduced by Mabel to Kauai. Years later Hotvedt said: [14]

> Miss Mabel was the promoter of the hospital project and largely carried the responsibility for it. She knew what pioneering involved. We always had her support and her patience was marvelous. Anna Williams, the administrator, had commenced her organization when I arrived. We did our planning and the paperwork at Grove Farm with frequent trips to Honolulu for purchasing. ... The department heads arrived later in the summer so then there were four of us at Grove Farm. Miss Mabel took us to the hospital and returned daily in her car.

More than a thousand people attended the dedication of the G. N. Wilcox Memorial Hospital on November 1, 1938, and two weeks later patients were transferred from the plantation hospitals in Kealia and Lihue, becoming Wilcox Hospital's first patients. There were 50 employees including four nursing supervisors, two head nurses, and eight registered nurses, all of them nursing school graduates.

Mabel and Elsie completed the dedication ceremony by simultaneously untying the *maile lei* stretched across the hospital door. The *Honolulu Star-Bulletin* singled out Mabel in its account, "It is given to few people to wield a more wide and helpful influence on the development of agencies for social welfare and true promotion of public and private medical and nursing standards than Miss Wilcox."

Chapter Thirteen

ON GOVERNING BOARDS

Mabel retired from public health nursing and administration in 1935, but that did not mean that she retired from the health care field. She continued to give equal attention and leadership to preventive health and acute care medicine attending many meetings as an officer of the G. N. Wilcox Memorial Hospital and Samuel Mahelona Memorial Hospital, and as president of the Kauai Tuberculosis Association and the Kauai Nurses Association. In 1950 she also was appointed to the Territorial Board of Health and regularly attended its monthly meetings in Honolulu.

The Wilcox Hospital was a business as well as a place for patient care. Mabel was treasurer, and she and the superintendent prepared regular financial reports of income and expenditures for the trustees. It was anticipated that patient fees would fall short of annual costs, and income from patients in 1939 ran 20 percent below operating requirements. As medical historian Charles Rosenberg has written of American voluntary hospitals in the early twentieth century, "In these years a deficit could be construed as a sign of worthiness and not a culpable failure." The financial deficit was made up by gifts from the G. N. Wilcox Trust, the S. W. Wilcox Trust and Elsie and Mabel Wilcox. The new hospital did not operate in the black until 1947.[1]

Hospital labor relations were a priority. Service workers unionized as part of the Construction and Service Workers' Union in 1947, and in 1952–1953 the hospital administration approved a 40-hour work week for nurses and office staff as well as for union members. An employee pension plan was created in 1954 for approximately 100 employees.[2]

The hospital was managed by Elizabeth Middleton, R.N., for 17 years. She had come to Kauai from a position as director of nursing and X-ray technician at Puunaiole Hospital in Hilo. Middleton had a wide range of experience, from working on a Big Island plantation to positions at hospitals in Peking, China and Cleveland, Ohio.

The key to Middleton's effectiveness as a hospital administrator was decisiveness and an excellent working relationship with the hospital's trustees, especially its Wilcox family members, G. P., Elsie, Mabel, and their nephew Sam, who joined the board in 1950. Middleton later compared the role of G. P. and Mabel in comments that said much about the uniqueness of the hospital board during her administration:

> They were both easy to work with. Miss Mabel never discussed much with me at the hospital except [as treasurer], but G. P. would come by once in ten days and sometimes once every week and sit down and talk with me for half an hour. He was really interested in the hospital, but I don't think anybody in the community ever realized what his interest was. ... One of the things that you noticed was that she was really very, very interested in the hospital as people, as persons, the personalities and how they fit in. And she'd tell you when she didn't think something was appropriate. She used to love it.[3]

Middleton gave her impressions of their individual styles as trustees:

> My experience with Miss Elsie was that she was a dominant person. And when my contacts with them were that—particularly on the board—Miss Mabel was treasurer of the hospital—but, Miss

Mabel, Gaylord, and Elsie shown at Gaylord's home, Kilohana, in the early 1950's.

Elsie, at board meetings, always dominated. Miss Mabel spoke of monetary things but never attempted to interfere in anything else that Miss Elsie had to say. She never disagreed with her—if she disagreed she never made any murmur on the subject, nor did G. P. After her death, the other two were quite outspoken about things—it was really quite amazing.

I felt that perhaps G. P. and Miss Mabel had got together before the meeting so that each one knew what they were going to carry and there was never any disagreement on the board, but you somehow had the feeling that one of them was pushing the particular issue, and the other would be just more or less in the background. ...

Well of course, Miss Elsie was a lot more talkative when she first met you, but it never stood up, she was always 'Miss Elsie', and you could call Mabel, 'Mabel'. And most of the time we didn't, we called her 'Miss Mabel', but even so, you could call her 'Mabel'; she was that friendly with most of the people that she knew at the hospital. But nobody ever took advantage of her. She never expected you to, and you didn't. But she'd love to have you come in; she'd love to have you go to the house and gossip. But Miss Elsie looked down on it.

Miss Mabel did a lot of very nice things for the employees. But nobody ever knew about them, and you know, when there were parties and all at the hospital, Christmas parties and that type of thing, she made contributions to them. And for a long time she came to the hospital Christmas parties, and thoroughly enjoyed them, and she knew all the old timers; course the new people didn't know her enough to appreciate what it all meant to have her come in. But nobody else, nobody else on the Board ever did any of that.[4]

Mabel took particular interest in the hospital's nurses. All eleven nurses first hired were graduates of hospital schools. It was part of the staffing standards that Mabel set, and Wilcox Hospital was the only acute care institution in the Islands to have its nursing staff entirely made up of training school graduates when it opened. Two Kauai women, Sueko Yamaura, R.N. and Martha Kumabe, R.N., had been trained at Queen's Hospital, and five other nurses had previous experience at Queen's or plantation hospitals. They all were helpful addressing the language and communication needs of local patients. Four of the nurses had been trained at the New York Woman's Hospital, Cook County Hospital in Chicago, Swedish Hospital in Seattle and

Kauai Nurses Association dinner to honor Mabel Wilcox in 1946 at Nurses' Home.

Highland Park Hospital in Michigan. The nurses all lived in the Nurses' Home along with the superintendent and took their meals together, or used the Nurses' Cottage at Poipu Beach for recreation. They attended meetings of the Kauai Nurses Association held at the hospital and at plantations. The monthly program topics chosen by Mabel included medicine and nursing, the sugar industry, and Hawaiian folklore. In 1942 at one of the meetings, Ethel Damon spoke about Hawaiian medicine and "augmented her talk with an exhibit at Grove Farm." Tsugie Kadota, R.N., said of Mabel: "I remember our Nurses Association Christmases at her home. What I remember about it was the Christmas tree with candles that she lit as we sat around the tree."[5]

Following the Japanese attack on Pearl Harbor, Wilcox Hospital and individual plantation hospital staffs coordinated efforts to prepare the island's population for possible Japanese bombing, shelling, and invasion, especially after a Japanese submarine shelled Nawiliwili Harbor in 1942. The hospital was painted in camouflage. The

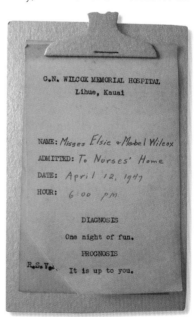

Invitation to "one Night of Fun" for Elsie and Mabel at Nurses' Home in 1947.

island hospitals, the Kauai Medical Society, and the Kauai Nurses Association worked with the Territorial Board of Health, Office of Civilian Defense, and the Red Cross to mobilize the community and bolster medical services for residents and for a large number of military personnel who started to arrive on Kauai in 1942. Outside the hospital Mabel was called upon to coordinate nursing services for the Office of Civilian Defense (O.C.D.), which together with the Army built and staffed several field hospitals to treat newly arrived troops. In addition, the hospitals were to be used for civilian evacuation in the event of an attack.[6]

Mabel took a personal interest in Wilcox Hospital's expanding maternal care. In the 1930s, before she retired, she had acknowledged the need for formal liaisons between Territorial nurses, plantation nurses, and local midwives; in 1934 she organized the first cooperative Territorial conference on Kauai, held in Hanapepe, where topics such as premature infant care, fetal complications, and syphilis in pregnancy were discussed. Adeline Mooklar, R.N., a new Territorial nurse who attended the conference remembered Mabel telling her,

Territorial Board of Health Bureau of Maternal and Child Health's first Midwife-Nurse Education Program, on Kauai, 1934. First row: (l to r) Guadalupe Besande, Andrea Santos, Maki Makimura, Konishi, Tsumoru Iwamoto, Mrs. Umeyo Oka, Cisco. Second row: (l to r) Nuncia Morris Bonilla, Mume Soo, unidentified, Mrs. Matsumoto, Mrs. Onitsuka. Back row: (l to r) unidentified, Doris Nishioka Hiramoto, Adeline Mooklar Deveruax, unidentified, Edith Moore, Claire Carra, Ethel Greathouse, Mabel Coleman, Mabel Wilcox.

"If you can't lick them, join them." The Second World War had the greatest impact on the practice of midwifery. Under martial law in Hawaii, all home deliveries ceased when births were required to take place in a hospital.[7]

By 1951 five out of seven newborns on Kauai were delivered annually at Wilcox Hospital. As birthing practices changed on the island, physician-assisted deliveries became the hospital's most important function.

Patricia L. Griffin's history, *Wilcox Memorial Hospital in the Twentieth Century*, describes how the hospital by the 1950s was "birthing at the seams." G. P., Elsie, and Mabel had been skeptical about raising money for an obstetrical wing, but Middleton told them that she thought it could be done and talked the trustees into going to the community for the first time to solicit funds for construction. In 1957 the new wing opened. It was dedicated to Elsie. She had died of cancer three years earlier.[8]

Mabel was busier than ever at the hospital. The trustees approved borrowing from the First National Bank of Hawaii to finance the building of an outpatient clinic when Lihue closed its dispensary a few years later. They also talked about seeking federal funds to pay for needed new acute care facilities. Philip Coke, who became hospital administrator in 1966, recalled:

> We had to build a new replacement facility. The Wilcoxes were all for it as long as I didn't get involved with government money. It was kind of humorous, because that was our only way out. We didn't have any funds, we had a cash flow shortfall, and we were really tottering at the point.

> The situation with the Hill Burton program then was that the Feds would match anything that the state supported. Obviously we had to compete with every other hospital including the state, to try to get funds. It became a real political issue. So I even had to get involved with the hospital association to make sure I was on the allocating council. So that state portion as you can imagine, was also political. And there were two legislators that helped us a lot: Billy Fernandez and Tony Kunimura. I must say, G. P. was willing to meet with those people—and he did an excellent job because I don't think he'd ever met with local legislators before, perhaps. They were overwhelmed and had great respect for both G. P. and Miss Mabel.[9]

Mabel Wilcox's Kauai Tuberculosis Association retirement photo taken at Grove Farm in 1949.

Mabel's contributions as an officer of the G. N. Wilcox Memorial Hospital and the Samuel Mahelona Memorial Hospital and as a director of the Kauai Tuberculosis and Health Association were examples of her continuing commitments to both clinical medicine and public health and the health care challenges they presented to her even after her retirement.

On the Mahelona board she served with Charles Rice, Jay Kuhns, M.D., Nobuichi Masunaga, M.D., Nicholas Akana, and Peter Kim, M.D., completing plans for a new 110-bed, publicly funded sanatorium in 1951. The new sanatorium was built because there still was a waiting list for hospital care on Kauai of those infected by tuberculosis. By the late 1950s, however, as Peter Kim, M.D., wrote, "it became apparent that drug treatment of tuberculosis had decreased the length of stay in hospital with the result that there were fewer patients remaining. ... The trustees recommended establishing a new program for the care of mentally ill to utilize the empty beds."[10]

Community health care problems on Kauai represented difficulties in integrating preventive and hospital services. Robert Worth, M.D., said that he talked easily with Mabel about public health problems like these, and he felt reassured by her professional and personal support. He cited one case in the late 1950s when he was the Kauai district health officer:

I think a classic story about the relationship between the hospital mainstream as embodied at Wilcox and public health was one episode, and Middleton played a role in it. One morning she called me up and told me that I should go follow up on what was happening at Hanamaulu School where they had an episode of gastroenteritis in the school kids. She got on to it because when she came to work that morning she found out that two little boys had come in with abdominal cramps and symptoms during the night. Both of them had been operated on for acute appendicitis, and one of them had died. The word was spreading like wildfire through the community that this was food poisoning, and in essence the school cafeteria had killed this little boy. So there was going to be a boycott. Nobody was going to eat anything from the cafeteria. The principal was all upset. The cafeteria manager and cook were about to commit suicide. It's interesting: Hanamaulu Village was part of Lihue Plantation, and Sam Wallis was the plantation doctor. But Middleton called me rather than Dr. Wallis, and that's the [hospital] mainstream deciding what it didn't want to mess with. So I got busy with the public health nurses and the sanitarians, and we worked our butts off for three days.

We interviewed everybody and took food histories and checked the milk and the water and the food to find out if it was anywhere else in the community, looked at absentee rates among the parents of these kids who were working in Lihue Plantation. It wasn't the food, and it wasn't the water. The kids who had taken their sandwiches from home had it just as much, and the cafeteria had it just as much as those who didn't drink milk. It wasn't the water supply because nobody in the village got it. It was just the kids in the school and their water line went to both places. You know, it was epidemiologically clear that it wasn't any of those things. So it couldn't have been the responsibility of the school, which made the principal very happy, but nobody believed it. So then the scene was to try and create a situation, persuade the parents that the cafeteria hadn't killed those kids. The most likely thing was that it was enterovirus spread by direct coughing and it was traceable to one sixth grader who had gone to Honolulu and had come back from visiting her cousins and got sick and went to school and was the school's messenger that day. Going to all the classrooms and it came down simultaneously in a short incubation period in every room except the kindergarten because she didn't go there. The kindergarten came in three days later.[11]

By this time in her life Mabel was also highly respected beyond Kauai. She still preferred to work behind the scenes on Kauai but was recognized off island for her many accomplishments. She enjoyed attending the once-a-year meetings of the Territory-wide Tuberculosis and Health Association on the different islands. Evelyn Mott-Smith, Kauai's Executive Secretary of the Association in the early 1950s recalled going to one such meeting on the Big Island:

> The young man who was the president of the Hilo Hawaii Association invited everyone up to his house for cocktails. They had a meeting in the afternoon and then he invited everybody up to his house, and then we had a meeting again in the evening and then the next morning people took off.

> Being an island boy from Hilo, he was just terrifically impressed that Miss Mabel was there. When we came in he ushered her into the parlor and had a chair ready for her and then he said "Now, Miss Mabel, I can get—we have ginger ale, we have 7-Up, we have Coke, we have soda water—what would you like?" She said, "I'd like a double scotch!"

Mabel attended her first national meeting of the Association in New York City and in Boston with Mott-Smith, who recalled their first day in Manhattan:

> Right away important people in New York started to call her. ... Someone from the United Nations who had been through and had a connection with Elsie, so [we] were invited to the U.N. for lunch. The head of the TB Association had us to the Harvard Club.

> In Boston, Miss Wilcox was involved with the higher echelon [while] I went to the various lectures and meetings. Then, pretty soon, she said "I've had it! Let's go on one of those tours! I've never been to a New England clambake, shall we go?" And I said 'Sure,' so about four o'clock one afternoon, we went to Salem and had a clambake and it smelled just like a *luau* ... anyway we sat there and ate until we were absolutely filled.[12]

PART IV 1960–1978

Chapter Fourteen

A DUAL LEGACY:
PRESERVING GROVE FARM

Mabel and Elsie took care of their Island home for as long as they lived, and towards the end of Mabel's career in nursing, public health, and hospital planning, she made a careful choice to prepare Grove Farm and its historical setting as an independent, non-profit museum.

The preservation of Grove Farm and its cultural identity was part of Mabel's purposeful legacy and is an example of women's contributions to the historic preservation movement. Her mental outlook represented pride in the past and complemented her contributions to "modernization". She acted on the premise that modernization was a process integrating heritage with economic and social change. She was an example of such integration, and it's fitting that Grove Farm stands as a testament to her legacy of caring.

In caring for Grove Farm and planning for its future, Mabel was one of the first preservationists in Hawaii to show that an historic house should retain a strong connection with its setting. She made it possible for Grove Farm's rural landscape, architecture, furnishings, works of art, Hawaiian artifacts, and historical library to receive equal preservation in their original location.

Grove Farm had been the center of Mabel and Elsie's professional world and home life since their births in the previous century. Hobey Goodale whose grandfather, Charles Rice, was a political rival of Elsie, recalls his experiences at the house with Mabel and Elsie's great niece Nancy:

> When Nancy and I announced our engagement Aunt Mabel said, "Why a Rice?" This was because of a political falling out between Aunt Elsie and Charles Rice, my grandfather. Well we got married

anyway. Aunt Mabel accepted me but would always make some small dig at me. I would just smile and get out of her way. Every Thanksgiving and Christmas Eve it was command performance for Nancy and I. Aunt Mabel tolerated me for two years. Finally at the third Thanksgiving Aunt Mabel came up to me and said, "Hobey, would you carve the turkey while I carve the ham." I knew then that I had passed muster and was now accepted into the family. After that Aunt Mabel could not have been more generous to my family and me.

In the 1930s, Mabel and Elsie had enjoyed their interests in history, literature, and the arts, and they strengthened their dedication to preserve Wilcox and Lyman family manuscripts, the plantation papers of G. N. Wilcox, and Abner Wilcox's original 600 acre pastureland at Lepeuli that they purchased from their uncle Albert's estate in 1935. It was a large and complex undertaking, but the Wilcox sisters were up to the task. As founders and benefactors of Waioli Mission House in Hanlei and the Lyman House Memorial in Hilo, they were in the tradition of other American women who played prominent roles in historic preservation by generating publicity, raising money, buying and restoring properties to save them, and collecting decorative arts.[1] Neither Mabel nor Elsie were reluctant to draw on the power of local government to help regulate land. Elsie had drawn up a lease to the

Waioli Mission House in Hanalei was restored by the three Wilcox sisters, Elsie, Etta and Mabel in 1921. Photo 1927.

County for maintaining acreage in front of Waioli Mission House as a large public park and community playing field.

In 1952 Mabel and Elsie formally incorporated Waioli Mission House as a family foundation, providing endowment income from rents and investments and choosing twelve of their nephews and nieces to be directors.[2] In those days if visitors happened upon Waioli, they might find a caretaker working in the yard, and the house might be unlocked for them to walk through the rooms. Waioli's annual meetings were held on the traditional Thanksgiving Day in the mission house.

Pam Wilcox Dohrman, Mabel's great niece, remembers:

As a child I recall my father Sam, Dick Sloggett, Sr., and the aunts attending the meeting. The purpose of the event was to tally the count of people and then open up the donation box and count the money donated by visitors to the Mission House. … Thanksgiving Dinner for the family followed the meeting at one of the family homes in Hanalei.[3]

Mabel and Elsie had developed their sense of preservation during travels to early American homes in New England and from G. N. and their parents' collecting interest at Grove Farm. Sam, Emma and G.N. made gifts of Hawaiian artifacts from Kauai to the Bernice Pauahi Bishop Museum on Oahu and helped the museum locate and restore a grass house or *hale pili* in 1890 for the new Hawaiian Hall. Committed to documenting their family's missionary history, Mabel and Elsie

Lyman House Memorial in Hilo, the childhood home of Emma Lyman Wilcox, was restored by Emma and her daughters, Elsie and Mabel in 1931.

privately printed two Wilcox history sources. The first was a collection of missionary letters written by their grandparents that had been found in Waioli Mission House. The letters were edited, with an interpretive narrative, by Ethel Damon. The correspondence contained insights into Abner and Lucy's spiritual life and household routines, as well as their work as teachers with Hawaiians at mission stations.

The second book was a genealogy, tracing the American Wilcox family from seventeenth-century Massachusetts, compiled by Elsie with help from her relatives in Connecticut and California and with assistance from a professional genealogist in New Haven.[4]

After Elsie's death in 1954, when Ethel Damon's own sister had passed away in Honolulu, Mabel invited Ethel to live with her at Grove Farm. They were comrades, and in many ways Ethel and been a member of the Wilcox family since the First World War when Mabel and Ethel served in France and Belgium. Ethel later stayed at Grove Farm while writing and editing her books; family members recalled Ethel's visits with Mabel and Elsie to Waioli, sometimes listening to her read aloud from Abner and Lucy Wilcox's letters on the kitchen *lanai*.

Old friends now in their 70s, Ethel and Mabel were still full of energy. Mabel flew to Honolulu once a month for Territorial Board of Health meetings, and Ethel, as a trustee of the Hawaiian Mission Children's Society, sometimes attended meetings. Ethel also completed her last book, a memoir of her missionary grandfather, Samuel Chenery Damon, in Grove Farm's conducive, familiar library surroundings.[5]

The Grove Farm home library also attracted some of younger Wilcoxes, and Mabel shared her knowledge of Hawaiiana and rare book collecting. One of her great-nephews, Sam Cooke, says that Mabel was his mentor and encouraged his collecting and the creation of his library in Honolulu. He remembers spending spare time in 1959 away from his hotel job in Lihue and learning from Mabel about bookseller John Howell in San

Mabel Wilcox and Ethel Damon at Maha-moku, Mabel's Hanalei beach house, which Mabel designed in 1915

Francisco, who helped Mabel and Elsie build their collection in the 1920s. Mabel and Elsie both felt that Kauai should have its own library of rare books on Hawaii. Their holdings included Hawaiian language books and first editions covering the early voyages and explorations by Cook, Vancouver, La Perouse, Kotzebue, and Wilkes.[6]

They believed that books on Hawaiian history were principal tools in education. Ethel and Elsie had hoped that a life story of G. N. Wilcox would be written as early as the 1930s. As the centennial of Grove Farm Company approached in the 1960s, Ethel and Mabel began planning the biography. Along with Mabel's brother Gaylord, who was president of the company, and William P. Alexander, a retired Grove Farm manager, they started to assemble archival materials about G. N. using the early plantation records housed in the old office building at the homestead. An invaluable primary source were the notes taken by Ethel of conversations she had with G. N. "In the evening," she said, "he'd sit there alone smoking in the library ... and he'd get to talking." She added, "He was interesting to the point of fascination, always accurate, often amusing and humorous."[7]

As research progressed, it was learned that the well-known Honolulu journalist, Bob Krauss, would be willing to recreate plantation scenes and vignettes from G. N.'s life, using the research materials at Grove Farm. The result was *Grove Farm Plantation: The Biography of a Hawaiian Sugar Plantation* by Bob Krauss and William P. Alexander, published by Grove Farm Company in 1965.

When Ethel was putting the final touches on the memoir of her grandfather, the Australian historian, Gavan Daws, tells of visiting Ethel and Mabel at Grove Farm when he was a University of Hawaii graduate student. Daws found Grove Farm to be a "restful sanctuary" and was intrigued by its sense of place and by the two women. He describes Grove Farm when Ethel lived there: "Pace of things totally leisurely, this partly so given the age of Mabel and Elsie, but as well, in the background was assurance that everything had been provided for, no hustle-bustle, worries, twitches." Daws continues:

> Mabel, while absolutely agreeable and effortlessly able to handle me, clearly had been and still was, a formidable woman: toughness, feistiness evident in her makeup. I remember her driving me back to the airport: small, small old lady, big, big, big car, forget what make—Mabel almost looking through rather than over the Detroit-size steering wheel. Driving at her own slow pace, with total assurance: nobody is about to run a Wilcox off the road.[8]

Ethel became ill and was in and out of the G. N. Wilcox Memorial Hospital a number of times until she passed away in 1965. It was a great loss to Mabel, who relied on Ethel in both public business and private matters. Geoffrey Michels, another of Mabel's cousins, told a story about her personality. On one occasion he was at lunch at Grove Farm with Mabel and Ethel while visiting from California. Michels told Mabel that he wanted to see the island of Niihau, presuming that she would arrange it for him. Mabel responded by telling him that Niihau belonged to the Robinson family; it was their island, and they chose not to have visitors. Michels felt chastised by Mabel, but Ethel took him aside on the *lanai* after lunch and told him: "Don't worry about it. She's never been invited to Niihau and is just dying to go too."[9]

Mabel's commitment to preservation moved into a new phase after Ethel's death with the arrival of Sophie Judd Cluff. Sophie, 30 years younger than Mabel, was recently widowed. The daughter of former Territorial Governor Lawrence M. Judd and a great-granddaughter of American Protestant missionaries, Sophie was keenly aware of Grove Farm's historical importance, its physical qualities as a *kamaaina*, or multi-generational, estate, and Mabel's belief that preservation would be best served if it was voluntary and privately supported.

Sophie wrote:

It was during many visits to Grove Farm from 1965 to 1967 to help Mabel with her Wilcox and Lyman manuscripts and her Hawaiian language books that she began confiding in me her hopes and dreams to preserve her beautiful home as a museum but didn't know how to go about it. Having been with the Mission Houses and its library for over ten years, being exposed to museum operations and having met many museum professionals, I began to think of ways to help her. By 1968 I had moved to Grove Farm to live with her.[10]

Sophie fully respected Elsie and Mabel's decision to keep G. N.'s sleeping quarters and his old plantation office filled with letterboxes, ledgers, and maps as they had been left in 1933. Sophie also was sensitive to preserving many everyday, common work routines at Grove Farm, and as an organic gardener she was drawn to the avocado and guava orchards, vegetable beds, flocks of chickens and ducks, and cattle grazing in the valley. Woodburning stove smoke rising out of the chimneys of the main house and laundry gave Sophie a deep sense of rural self-sufficiency, engendered by her daily walks around Grove Farm and observations of Mabel's household staff and *luna* Alberto Daguay.

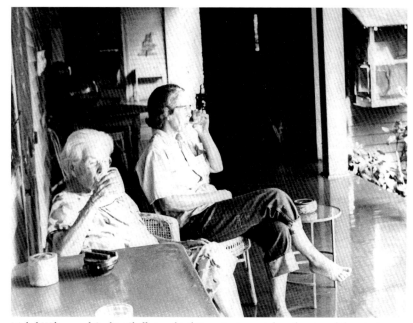

Mabel Wilcox and Sophie Cluff at cocktail time sipping scotch and water while enjoying cigarettes on the Grove Farm lanai overlooking Nawiliwili Valley in the early 1970's.

Robert Schleck, who came to work at Grove Farm in the 1970s, becoming the museum's first curator, observes that, "It was totally as a result of Sophie's encouragement and drive that Miss Mabel even considered undertaking such a monumental effort at that point in her life." He adds,

> Sophie's arrival was the turning influence in its preservation. While many family members joined to help with the museum project, the effort did not take life until her arrival. Miss Mabel seemed to embrace it once Sophie committed herself. Sophie had a great dramatic flare that could fire people's imaginations and enjoyed awakening their interest in and awareness of history.[11]

Sophie's first major project at Grove Farm was to help Mabel make arrangements for a donation of her Hawaiiana books and other publications in the Grove Farm library to the State of Hawaii. For many years, Mabel and Elsie had let it be known that they intended to give their private collection to the State of Hawaii for a "research library of Hawaiiana for the island of Kauai." Formal discussions began in 1968 in a meeting with Mabel, Sophie, James Hunt (director of the Hawaii State Library), Janet Bell (director of the Sinclair Library at the University of Hawaii), and Thelma Hadley (director of the Kauai Public

Library).[12] A new public library in Lihue was under construction; it was agreed there would be a separate room for the Elsie and Mabel Wilcox collection. Specific provisions for security, care of books, and rules for access by readers were developed and incorporated in the deed of the gift. Mabel's first donations to the new library were made in 1969 and consisted of Bernice P. Bishop Museum publications. Over the next ten years she gave more than 1,600 rare books about Hawaii and the Pacific to the new library, where Sophie Cluff catalogued the collection in the 1980s. Mabel's duplicate copies remained shelved at Grove Farm, and there was an agreement that became significant twenty-five years later. Should the State be unable to maintain the collection, the public library would return custody and ownership of the books to Mabel. It couldn't and in 1995 the books were returned to Grove Farm.[13]

Mabel may have thought she was back in her busy hospital planning days. "With my urging," Sophie wrote later, "she began discussing the possibility of a museum with her nephews Sam Wilcox and Dick Sloggett. Sam thereupon took up ownership, tax, and endowment problems." Mabel only had lifetime residency on the homestead according to her uncle's will, after which the property would revert to Grove Farm Company family stockholders. Mabel made an offer to buy nearly 80 acres, the main house and all surrounding structures. The family understood that she would bequeath her estate to the new museum she was creating. The Grove Farm Company shareholders voted almost unanimously to give Mabel a purchase option, and she had an appraisal prepared.[14]

Mabel's support for the preservation of Grove Farm and the assistance she enlisted from others in historical research, building and artifact conservation, and planning soon became a vital part of her lifetime legacy—an addition to Mabel's already, impressive, unprecedented, career.

Her bequest was to include sufficient endowment funds to help with future maintenance and operations, but her nephews were concerned about the effect of new federal tax changes whereby family-supported private foundations like Waioli would be taxed heavily. At the suggestion of the director of the American Association of Museums, Mabel decided to go beyond her Honolulu attorneys, and she retained the services of an Ohio lawyer, Robert Bromberg, who specialized in tax-exempt regulations. He played a key role in the Grove Farm museum. Bromberg's early recommendations included broadening the Waioli Board of Trustees to make it more representative of the community;

seeing that ten percent of Waioli's annual income was raised from the public; and creating a legal framework for a "subsidiary, tax-exempt museum organization that would develop and manage Grove Farm through the use of Mabel's endowment funds and to provide additional funds to maintain Waioli Mission House." The charitable purpose of the subsidiary to preserve, maintain and operate historical property was similar to Waioli's charitable purpose.[15]

Mabel was familiar with conventional examples of house museums associated with the lives of political leaders, wealthy merchants, writers, and poets, and she realized that her ideas for Grove Farm in the 1960s were part of what historian Michael Kammen has described as "an astounding increase in the number of new institutions as well as the expansion of museums in general and historical museums in particular."[16] Sophie also understood from her experience at the Hawaiian Mission Children's Society how important it was for documents and other collections to be accessible to serious scholars. Mabel and Sophie gave Professor Edward Beechert at the University of Hawaii permission to study the Grove Farm plantation labor records after he made a research request. Beechert remembered his first visit:

> I was sent off to the Plantation office with the key. Opening the door and stepping in was like going in to a time machine. I almost expected the bookkeeper to come to the desk and resume work. It was an amazing scene. Looking at the files and letters was exciting. Here were the pieces of a working plantation—all the details of day to day operations.

What Mabel and Sophie learned as their planning picked up speed was that historic preservation was coming of age. State historic preservation archaeology surveys contributed to a deeper understanding of Hawaiian culture; the ambitious architectural restoration and refurnishing of Iolani Palace was encouraged by National Park Service Historic American Buildings Survey architects like Charles Peterson; commercial rehabilitation of Chinatown in Honolulu saved many vernacular urban buildings; the memories of local residents in Chinatown and ethnic groups elsewhere in the Islands were being recorded by oral history projects; and it was obvious that the collections at Grove Farm were of interest to museum curators, art historians, and bibliographers working in Hawaii. Nostalgia for the sugar industry and plantation social history was growing, as symbolized by Waipahu Cultural Park on Oahu. For the Wilcox family, planning the Grove Farm museum became an opportunity to build on the company's centennial and celebrate G. N.'s life. As Pam Dohrman said, "he amassed a fortune during his lifetime in the sugar industry. He used his money to care for others, first in his family, his plantation, and then the people of Kauai and Hawaii. Similarly, Aunty Mabel was taught to tend, and to care for and give to people."[17]

It was a time of growing professionalization in Hawaii's museums. The Hawaii Museums Association was founded in 1968 and almost overnight the organization became a clearinghouse and sounding board for museum staff and trustees. The practice and challenges of new research and interpretation were discussed at meetings and in consultation with representatives of mainland groups, particularly the programs of the American Association for State and Local History, and field services provided by the National Trust for Historic Preservation.[18]

Mabel, Sophie, and Dick Sloggett participated in and supported the Hawaii Museums Association's early semi-annual meetings, Sophie regularly calling upon Jane Silverman, the Hawaii State Parks historian, for museum and preservation advice. Jane suggested that Mabel and Sophie invite George Moore, a museum specialist working for the State of Hawaii, to visit Kauai to make recommendations about turning Grove Farm into a museum.[19]

On his first visit, Moore discussed standard museum operations: collections management, cataloguing and registration, space for storage, and the conservation of collections, and he introduced the museum "team" to Carl E. Guthe's useful *The Management of Small Museums*.

Mabel agreed that Moore should return to Grove Farm to meet with a newly formed committee of family members, providing the committee with a written report including a sketch map of proposed uses of existing buildings that reflected several new acquisitions.

Mabel accepted plantation equipment and blacksmith tools from the Waipouli shop of E. H. W. Broadbent, G. N.'s longtime manager, and one idea was to reconstruct the shop at the homestead. Future gifts included historical 16 mm films made by Digby Sloggett, G. N. Wilcox's nephew, and the camp house furnishings of Kikuni Moriwaki, the longtime laundress, after her death. Grove Farm Company was willing to make a gift of its four narrow-gauge steam locomotives. These engines were stored at the plantation roundhouse in Puhi and were no longer in use after Grove Farm closed its 14-mile rail line in the 1950s, trucks replacing the older form of transportation. One of the steam engines in storage was "Paulo," manufactured in 1887 in Germany and shipped to Koloa Sugar Company. It was the oldest surviving plantation locomotive in the Islands and had become an icon of the industry on Kauai since display at the Koloa plantation centennial in 1935.

William M. Moragne, Grove Farm Company's manager, wrote to the manager of Hamakua Mill Company, "In talking to Miss Wilcox the other day, it was apparent that she is anxious to construct the equipment used in the Hawaiian sugar industry, dating all the way back to the stone mills."[20]

"First things first" is probably what Sophie thought, considering the conservation jobs already waiting at the homestead. Repairs to buildings began in 1970 when the restoration architects for Iolani Palace, Geoffrey Fairfax and Blaine Cliver, were asked to make measured architectural drawings of Grove Farm and to carefully supervise much-needed repairs for three overgrown, deteriorating buildings: the tea house, fernery, and an old shed.

The family, including Mabel, continued to help in various ways. Sam Wilcox and his wife Edie made a long trip through New England, visiting house museums and historic places, including Historic Deerfield, the Essex Institute, Shelburne Museum, and Mystic Seaport. They called on a cousin in rural Brookfield, Vermont, and thanks to the Litchfield Historical Society, they located the old Wilcox farmhouse in Harwinton, Connecticut. Sam and Edie were well traveled in Britain, Europe, and Japan, but Edie thought the New England trip with its many family association was the best trip that she ever took."[21]

Mabel first informed the County Planning Commission about the future museum in 1971. With Sophie's help she wrote:

> We think that Grove Farm Homestead—once the site of Grove Farm Plantation—can be developed into a living restoration that can tell the story of a sugar plantation and of George Norton Wilcox, the man who developed it and of the Sam Wilcox family who lived here, of the agricultural and technological aspects, and of the human relationships of literally thousands of people of all races who were linked with Grove Farm Plantation since 1864. This is a unique site, one that has unlimited educational prospects, and one that is well known because of the recently published book.

Alarmed by a state highway plan to bypass Nawiliwili Harbor to the airport by cutting directly through the homestead valley, Mabel invited the mayor and county commissioners to visit Grove Farm in person. They accepted. Mabel wrote:

It is my hope that the homestead, comprising approximately 78 acres, will be preserved in its entirety. This will ensure space to develop our story in such a way that neither spatial nor aesthetic inhibitions will be forced upon the site; it will help protect the historic landscape from incursion by commercial and other developments inconsonant with the living restoration; and it will provide valuable open space that will enhance the environmental aspects of a growing community.[22]

Sophie wrote Geoffrey Fairfax: "Well, the 'fat is in the fire.'"

The year after Mabel celebrated her 90th birthday, Sophie wrote Jane Silverman:

"Great occasion, happy one, exciting too—beautiful flowers, many b'day cards, am now busy writing thank-u notes for Miss Mabel. She invited her nieces & nephews and their adult children plus plantation officers, about 40 in all, for "open house," everyone commented on what a very special feeling was felt."[23]

With so much preservation work to do, Mabel realized she needed more help. Robert Schleck was employed and Sophie wrote to Jane:

Bob Schleck started work for Miss Mabel Oct. 2nd, is a great worker, does anything, even mopped office bldg floors this a.m. to prepare for some trust meetings there tomorrow! Actually is doing mostly accessioning rite now, tho I shift him about to relieve the tedious work. … Best thing about him is that he sees things that need to be done without waiting to be told, is quiet and unobtrusive but

Robert Schleck working on the inventory of Mabel Wilcox's Grove Farm home in 1972, in preparation for her plantation museum.

creative and steady. I just hope he'll progress up the ladder of museumology and not be wooed away by the [Kauai] museum later on.[24]

Bob recalls that he first started on Saturday mornings:

It is my impression that the Saturday project was a way to determine if I would fit into the life of the house, given that there had not been

"Peahi o Kaiulani" – Kaiulani's Fan, one of thirty-five Hawaiian quilts collected by Elsie and Mabel Wilcox.

a man involved there on a fulltime basis since G. N. died in 1933. Interestingly, many of the household operations were done by men during G. N. and Sam's time ... after their deaths women did all the inside operations.[25]

Hisae Mashita, who had been the cook in 1936, told Bob that when he first started on Saturday the housekeepers "were on their morning break having been summoned by Hisae leaning out the kitchen back door and ringing the brass school hand bell." One of them said, "Who's that *haole* boy?" Bob says that he learned about Mabel's preservation philosophy in practical ways:

A pivotal experience in my involvement at Grove Farm was when Harold Rosa was clearing magnolia leaves from the gutter by the kitchen, which was part of his monthly routine. Understanding that

The "Welcome" rug at Waioli Mission House is one of twenty hooked rugs collected by Mabel Wilcox.

Sophie was always looking for ways to cut costs of the operation of Grove Farm, I turned to Miss Mabel, who was standing watching him, and said, "If we put chicken wire over the gutter, it would keep the leaves out and eliminate the need for this." Her response was, "Wait until I'm gone before you do that." It entirely changed my approach to the place, now understanding that the function was historical and therefore needed to be preserved.[26]

One of Schleck's first jobs was to study the furnishing and collection inventory records made by Elsie and to introduce a museum registration system suggested by Thomas Frye, Curator of History at the Oakland Museum, after a visit to Grove Farm. Schleck notes:

> I was entirely focused on the inventory project, looking for guidance from a variety of sources from local historic house museums, to Tom Frye of the Oakland Museum, and a variety of house museums on the mainland. The consistent response from everyone was that I needed to develop my own system, following a basic format which Tom Frye had provided.[27]

Grove Farm was listed in the National Register of Historic Places in 1972. The homestead was recommended as "an associational site that documents G. N. Wilcox's accomplishments," and Sophie cooperated with Jane Silverman, now the Hawaii State Historic Preservation Officer, and her staff with preparation of the nomination. Jane continued to offer preservation advice and suggested that Barnes Riznik should be invited to visit Grove Farm and Waioli during my vacation to the Islands in 1973.

> I was then vice president for museum administration at Old Sturbridge Village in Massachusetts. Silverman was familiar with Sturbridge Village because of the year she spent at the large outdoor history museum in Massachusetts as part of a cooperative American history graduate study program, directed by the University of Connecticut.[28]

> I toured the homestead with Sophie, Bob Schleck, and Jane Silverman and was asked many questions about house museum practices and planning. Mabel was an interested participant in conversations over several days at both Grove Farm and Waioli, which we visited together. Like others seeing Grove Farm for the first time, I was intrigued by the many collections I saw: the rare books and works of art; Hawaiian artifacts; the many records kept in G. N.'s old office; plantation structures that had been designed and built one by one as they were needed; a whole world of everyday plantation resources still in use by the gardeners and household staff: from a rain gauge, to the functioning iron cooking range in the kitchen, to the number of exceptional trees, kitchen gardens, and most of all, I thought, the land itself that continued to produce food. I was interested in other things in the house: the reminders of Elsie Wilcox's political career

and her many contributions to the Kauai Historical Society. I found Mabel's public health nurse's cottage, with her professional library on tuberculosis, maternal and infant care and other forms of preventive medicine, saved in the separate building along with her records. Grove Farm had much to tell about women's history. I realized that the lives of the two sisters were as significant as their uncle's, and that the home documented their contributions as well as G. N.'s and represent an amalgamation of the interests of successive family generations. There were only a few other places like Grove Farm preserved anywhere in the United States.

Mabel and Sophie were interested in my reactions to Grove Farm and their proposed visitor tour routes and a site layout. They specifically expressed their concerns about how much walking visitors from Honolulu and the mainland might be expected to do but based upon my experience at Stubridge Village and elsewhere I observed:

> I'm very aware of persons living in our society who are self-conscious about space. When they see a way of life in which land was used to support an economy, they want to get out into it. They've been boutiqued to death if they have urban experiences … don't worry at all about encouraging people to really go some distance … people go to botanical gardens and walk their legs off. I think you can do it here with historic houses and properties.[29]

The two ladies talked about the sequences of visiting buildings and areas, and Mabel asked, "Don't most people want to see the house first, and then go out into the agriculture?" I suggested:

> No one ever has [all] the answers in historic house interpretation, but if it's Grove Farm, you have potential here that a typical historic house museum does not have—land and outbuildings … historic interpretation of land use and the family's evolution over a century or more on this site. … I think the house can be most powerful as a culminating experience which ties together the evolution of the family. … To come upon it in its maturity, its sophistication, and your own family's taste as reflected in the furnishings is best midway through and not at the start.[30]

Mabel wanted to discuss this point. "The family of course started the thing, that's why my feeling was that most people want to see the house and why the family developed, and they developed all that area out there that you start us on. … I don't know … I'm glad to hear the other." I pointed out that Grove Farm was an "incomparable experience," Monticello coming to mind: "You come upon a hill and you are aware of how much land Jefferson had. You see the house in the distance. You're directed into the supporting buildings first and then tour the house." Sophie added, "It can always be flexible."[31]

Sophie showed a layout, prepared by the architects, of various locations for display of additional plantation tools and equipment, including a locomotive. She told me that it had been suggested that "if you wanted a separate blacksmith shop it might be feasible to have a little building in here—if the traffic were coming this way through the shed and out and then through the blacksmith shop." Sophie said that she felt that its display might be inappropriate:

> There wasn't a blacksmith shop at all ... and we had toyed with the idea of the locomotives, but there's no space here and it would clutter and would need too tremendous an area.[32]

I agreed. "That's what so many [museum] people have done for the last 50 years. Bringing things in you can get a stifled feeling. You jam irrelevant objects right at the edge of a setting, and it loses its organic being. You talk about organic farming, there's also an organic landscape. ... You put the locomotive too close to the visitor's initial experience, he's going to think that locomotives is all you're about." Later, when the plans were discussed with Mabel she said, "The [suggestion] didn't particularly appeal to me, so I'm glad you said that." Sam Wilcox added to the discussion that he thought Grove Farm was like an English county house where everything is preserved just as it was centuries ago.[33]

At the end of the first day I could not help but think about Grove Farm as a place of discovery and wonder. Several new ideas for the future came out of my visit. Jane Silverman and I encouraged the acquisition of Kaipu Camp, a group of small single-family worker's cottages contiguous to Mabel's estate that were rented by Grove Farm Company to employees. I explained:

> I would like to keep these buildings standing because as a group they are probably unique or will get to be unique, a good example of a row of plantation houses. If they can be maintained so people can live in them, you are going to have to deal with certain modern intrusions—TV, autos ... main thing is to keep these things going and to get these into the plan even though it is the modern re-use of buildings.

It is very rare to find [remaining] industrial workers' housing and they should be kept from being demolished.[34] Mabel later told Bob Schleck that the idea of the preservation of Kaipu Camp at Grove Farm was "a revolution in her mind"—a new perspective for a woman who had spent so much of her career visiting various plantation homes as they pertained to public health. [35]

I was most impressed during my visit with Mabel, Sophie, and the others by the tangible presence of another era. Grove Farm just felt *lived in*. Familiar as I was with effective new methods of museum "living history" and "role playing" at Plimoth Plantation, Old Sturbridge Village, and the National Park Service, Grove Farm seemed to have authenticity of its own—thanks to Mabel, Elsie, and their uncle.

Sophie recorded our discussions, which I have excerpted here. At earlier times she had taped Mabel's recollections of her brothers and sisters and growing up at Grove Farm, but Mabel was shy when talking about herself. Jane then suggested that Sophie arrange for a videotape interview with Mabel at Grove Farm by Hawaii Public Television. Sophie understood how important this was, and somehow she convinced Mabel to go on camera with Bob Barker, the director of the Hawaii Public Television series "Pau Hana," who taped her for broadcast television on January 26, 1973. Mabel talked with Barker in the living room, kitchen, and outside in the tea house gazebo.

Sophie wrote to Jane:

Must tell you that Mabel was wonderful on the TV interview, tho she balked at the idea and was "furious" at me for asking her to do it, but once she got going w/Barker, she loosened up and sparkled and I do hope that sparkle and laughter will come through on the show. ...

Spent the last two days chatting w/her, got most on tape, so I could jot down "leading" questions and notes for Barker ... Gorgeous morning, now a rainy aft. They worked until 12:30, interviewed her first on the sofa, then out to kitchen stool, by wood stove, then out to tea house, ended by Barker & Mabel walked "off into the sunrise" from house toward pasture, and the mango trees in tremendous blossom added all kinds of color. In between each interview, which last about 10 min, she would relax and smoke like mad and rest, while he lined up a few questions and leads.

I think it will be great.[36]

The Grove Farm locomotives were stored in Puhi at the roundhouse next to the Grove Farm Company shops. Mabel and Sophie decided to restore a locomotive and have it run it under steam at Puhi. Sophie contacted the Hawaii Railway Society. It recommended Matt Austin, a

1975 Once Mabel Wilcox began work on her museum plans for Grove Farm, her annual Christmas card highlighted her major project of the year. In 1975, her christmas card (shown above) recorded her at the celebration of her restoration of "Wainiha", one of four sugar locomotives given to her for her museum by Grove Farm Company.

young mechanical engineering student, to do the job with help from Grove Farm staff. In 1975, "Wainiha," one of the Baldwin engines, was selected for the nine-month project. Interest in the restoration was widespread on Kauai, and it peaked at the rededication celebration. An unpublished account exists in the literary papers of the author Kathryn Hulme. A friend of Mabel and Sophie, she captured the color, personality, and emotion of the event and showed that there was as much about the excitement over Mabel's plans to preserve Grove Farm as about "Wainiha's" big day.

Kate Hulme wrote:

The waiting crowd composed mainly of plantation men and their families had dressed casually for the celebration—the men in aloha shirts and the women in bright muumuus or pant suits, fine for color photography in the silvery light of that November afternoon. Everyone knew everyone and while waiting for Miss Mabel to appear, they photographed each other against the background of the tall roundhouse doors painted white for the occasion. Only the grandchildren of this plantation hierarchy showed eagerness; occasionally they ran up to peer through the crack of the double doors to see what was going on in the great gloom of a locomotive roundhouse.

Presently Miss Mabel appeared without fanfare. Her blue sedan moved quietly through the crowd to a vacant space in the front row of the roundhouse audience, just where an opera box might have been located had this been a theatrical presentation—which in a way it was. Seated beside her driver, who was a tall, spectacled descendant of the Judd missionary clan and presently official archivist of Grove Farm and companion to Miss Mabel, Miss Mabel herself appeared smaller and more fragile than she actually was.

Over the loudspeaker came the locomotive's genealogy: "Grove Farm Number 6 or 'Wainiha' as we know her was ordered by Alexander & Baldwin for McBryde Sugar Company in 1915." The long list of her restorers was read out—the men who had put her together piece by piece, welded, hammered and painted her and polished all her brasswork, especially her great bell. At the mention of her bell, we suddenly heard its deep-throated clang echoing under the iron eaves of the engine barn. It was a slow tolling, a sound musical and brief as someone in the engine cab must have tugged gently on the bell rope and then had let go.

The real show was about to begin. "Wainiha stood stock still for an instant, then suddenly she let out a blast from her steam whistle, a hoot of triumph accompanied by a rush of white steam as she broke from her roundhouse sequestering and began to back onto

A corner in the 1915 parlor, showing the double portrait of Sam and Emma Wilcox painted by Charles Bartlet in 1929. Arranged below it is a koa gate-leg table, Sam's upholstered armchair and Emma's koa rocking chair. The koa furniture was made at the Hilo Boarding School.

Grove Farm library as arranged by Elsie and Mabel Wilcox for their Hawaiian book collection.

her narrow-gauge stage under her own power for the first time in eighteen years.

Yards of fresh flower leis garlanded her from cab front to cow-catcher, looped around her round black belly and festooning her steam whistle. When she had backed fully into view, clanging and fuming, with great clouds of smoke and steam blowing out from chimney stack and fireboxes and her whistle that could be heard a half-mile away, she paused for a moment before Miss Mabel's parked car as if making a bow to her restorer. [37]

Mabel retired as president of the Waioli Board of Trustees in 1974, and Richard Sloggett was elected to take her place. The board was expanded with seven community leaders in education, conservation, library administration, and business invited to join the five family members. The Trustees were Gale Carswell, Sophie Cluff, Ralph Daehler, Pam Beck, Clyde French, Donna Marie Garcia, Nancy Goodale, Gabriel I, Winona Sears, Dick Sloggett, Sam Wilcox, and Maili Yardley.

Thus, it was the new job of the trustees to establish the policies for managing what would become endowment funds, design research and education programs, select the full-time museum director, and create support on Kauai and elsewhere that would take Grove Farm public. Looking to the past and future, they began to operate on their own within the scope of Mabel's preservation legacy. [38]

Mabel died in December 1978 at Grove Farm at the age of 96. After the graveside service, she was buried on the hillside at Lihue Cemetery next to her parents, Uncle George, and her sisters and brothers.

Her legacy survives in the ongoing development of health care on Kauai and in the preservation of Waioli Mission House, Lyman Memorial Museum, Grove Farm and all their stories.

Grove Farm lanai in 2004. (Photo courtesy Colonial Homes)

Exterior of Grove Farm main house in 2004.

Acknowledgements

I met Mabel Wilcox and Sophie Cluff in 1973 as their guest at Grove Farm when I was invited to discuss their museum plans. Everything in the house breathed of the past. I first learned of Mabel Wilcox's significant contributions to health care and nursing reforms there and saw her preservation of Grove Farm's library, plantation records and Wilcox family papers. Primary source documentation included Mabel Wilcox's correspondence, reports and photographs spanning the 50 years of her career. Her life impressed me, as it did so many others; her presence was felt everywhere on Kauai as a public health nurse, hospital builder and remarkable woman.

Her life interested me for other particular reasons. Ten years earlier, I had made a study of the history of the professional lives of early nineteenth-century New England doctors for the Research Department at Old Sturbridge Village in Massachusetts. Catherine Fennelly from the Sturbridge days and Lloyd Stevenson, then editor of the Journal of the *History of Medicine and Allied Sciences,* deserve special appreciation for encouraging my research interest in health care.

I was extremely fortunate to be appointed Director of Waioli Mission House and Grove Farm museum in 1976. My work on this book began with the museum's preparation of an archival guide to the Grove Farm sugar plantation records and the Wilcox family papers and a subsequent, extensive oral history of the lives of nurses and other health professionals. I am especially indebted to Becky O'Leary for her preparation of the archival aids and to Ruth Smith for her skilful interviews. The projects were supported in part by grants from the National Endowment for the Humanities and the G.N. Wilcox Trust.

The biography would not have progressed without the help of Robert Schleck, the Director of Waioli Mission House and Grove Farm museums. From his organization and care of the museum's collections to his choice of the illustrations for the book, assisted by the museums' Curator, Moises Madayag, Bob has been and continues to be a wonderful colleague. Similarly, Ruth Smith, who became a Waioli Mission House and Grove Farm museum Trustee, has made supportive suggestions about the book and was a careful reader while providing leadership for the museum. I am very grateful to her.

I am also indebted to librarians, archivists, curators and public health officers in Hawaii and on the Mainland who provided me with help especially Margaret Lovett at the Kauai Museum; Margery Hastert and Helen Wong Smith at The Queen's Medical Center; John Breinich and his staff at the Hawaii Medical Library; Dr. Richard K. C. Lee: Dr. Robert Melton; Ann Marsteller at the Hawaii Agriculture Research Center (formerly known as the Hawaii Sugar Planters' Association); Agnes Conrad and Susan Shaner at the Hawaii State Archives; Stephanie Long at Dana Hall School; and Gerard Shorb at the Alan Mason Chesney Medical Archives, Johns Hopkins Medical Institutions.

Recent scholarship in the social history of American medicine, nursing, Hawaiian culture, ethnic history and sugar plantations has produced invaluable new articles and books that have informed perspectives on Mabel Wilcox's life. Several historians most generously gave their time and detailed reviews of many drafts: Edward Beechert, Richard Candee, Jane Silverman and Judith Hughes. Judy provided new scholarship from her own biographical study of Mabel Wilcox's sister, Elsie Wilcox. Pat Griffin also suggested many leads and interpretive ideas from her history of the G. N. Wilcox Memorial Hospital. Bob Krauss and Jan TenBruggencate generously shared their years of experience writing about Grove Farm's history.

I offer special thanks to Tara Bray Smith for editing the manuscript in its final stages of preparation with sensitive literary skill, keeping my focus on Mabel Wilcox in all the chapters. I am also appreciative of word processing by Patricia Palama and Jennifer Almeida from my very rough drafts.

This book about Mabel Wilcox's character and experiences also benefited greatly from conversations with members of her family, particularly Nancy and Hobey Goodale, Richard and Anna Sloggett, Edie Wilcox, Geoffrey Wilcox Michels, Pam Dohrman, Patsy Sheehan and

Gaylord Wilcox and Sam Cooke. Marion Penhallow and Beryl Blaich are also to be thanked for their contributions.

Finally, my deepest words of gratitude are for my wife, Ba. This book not only might never have been completed without her, it might never even have begun.

Thank you all.

Osterville, Massachusetts

March, 2005

Notes

Introduction

1. Mabel L. Smyth, "Public Health Nursing in Hawaii: A Tribute to Mabel I. Wilcox," *The Pacific Coast Journal of Nursing*, vol. 31, no. 6 (June, 1935) 297-298. Ethel M. Damon, "Mabel Wilcox, Pioneer in Public Health," *Paradise of the Pacific Annual*, 1952, 26-28; Margaret M.L.Catton, *Social Serice in Hawaii* (Pacific Books: Palo Alto, 1959), 146-148: Frances R. Hegglund Lewis, *History of Nursing in Hawaii* (German Kilmer Co.: Node, Wyoming, 1969), 119-122. See also Mary Cooke, "Miss Mabel of Grove Farm," *The Sunday Star-Bulletin and Advertiser*, October 31, 1965; television interview, "Pau Hana Years," January 26, 1973, Hawaii Public Television.

2. Bob Krauss and William P. Alexander, *Grove Farm Plantation: The Biography of a Hawaiian Sugar Plantation* (Pacific Books: Palo Alto, 1965, 1984).

3. Mark Caldwell, *The Last Crusade: The War on Consumption, 1862-1954* (Atheneum: New York, 1988). Chapter 2: " 'The Greatest Battle Ever Fought'."

4. Smyth, "Public Health Nursing in Hawaii," 298; Damon, "Mabel Wilcox, Pioneer in Public Health," 27; Richard A. Meckel, *Save the Babies: American Public Health Reform and the Prevention of Infant Mortality, 1850-1929* (The Johns Hopkins University Press: Baltimore, 1990). Chapter 5: "Better Mothers, Better Babies, Better Homes."

5. Griffin, Pat L., *Wilcox Memorial Hospital in the Twentieth Century* (Wilcox Health Foundation: Lihue, 2000). ix-xv.; Rosemary Stevens, *In Sickness and In Wealth: American Hospitals in the Twentieth Century,* (Basic Books: New York, 1989). Chapter 1, "Introduction."

6. Mabel Wilcox, unpublished paper, "Personal Report of Service with the Red Cross," 1919. Mabel I. Wilcox Papers. GFM; John van Schaick, *The Little Corner Never Conquered: The Story of the American Red Cross War Work for Belgium* (Macmillan: New York, 1922.) Chapter 23: "Dr. Park's Great Experiment."

7. Kerr L. White, *Healing the Schism: Epidemiology, Medicine, and the Public's Health* (Springer-Verlag: New York, 1991) Chapter 9: "Back to the Future." The public health historian Elizabeth Fee clarifies this issue further: "Medicine and public health are intimately related, often overlapping. and yet they also have contradictory interests. Public health is oriented towards the analysis of the determinant of health and disease on a population basis, while medicine is oriented toward individual patients." Elizabeth Fee, *Disease and Discovery: A History of the Johns Hopkins School of Hygiene and Public Health, 1916-1939* (The Johns Hopkins University Press: Baltimore, 1987) 1-8.

8. "Kauai Public Health Oral History Project," interviews conducted by Ruth Smith, 1982-1985, 42 transcripts. Grove Farm Museum; Mabel I. Wilcox Papers are described in Margaret R. O'Leary, comp. *Register of the Grove Farm Plantation Records and Papers of George N. Wilcox, Samuel W. Wilcox, Emma L. Wilcox, Elsie H. Wilcox and Mabel I. Wilcox*; Ellen Conliffe Legemann, ed. *Nursing History: New Perspectives, New Possibilities*, (Teachers College Press: New York, 1983), Chapter 1: "Introduction."

Chapter One: **When Two Worlds Met**

1. Emma Wilcox to Sarah Lyman. November 3, 1882. Samuel W. Wilcox and Emma L. Wilcox Papers, Grove Farm Museum (GFM).

2. Emma Wilcox to Sarah Lyman, November 23, 1882. GFM. Emma Lyman was born at Hilo, the youngest child of the Reverend and Mrs. David B. Lyman, American missionaries. She was married to Samuel Wilcox on October 7, 1874. Wilcox was born at Waioli, one of missionary Abner Wilcox and Lucy Wilcox's eight sons. St. David Gynlais Walters was born in Wales, educated at Cambridge University and Edinburgh University medical school. Walters was appointed government physician

for Lihue by the Board of Health in 1881 and also opened an office in Lihue where he practiced for 15 years. See typescript "In Memorium: Doctors of Hawaii." Hawaii Medical Library.

3. *Ibid.*

4. Ethel M. Damon, ed. *Letters from the Life of Abner and Lucy Wilcox, 1836-1869* (Privately published: Honolulu, 1950) 166.

5. Patricia Grimshaw, *Paths of Duty: American Missionary Wives in Nineteenth-Century Hawaii* (University of Hawaii Press: Honolulu, 1989) 94. The lives of Lucy Wilcox and Sarah Lyman as missionary wives and mothers confirmed Grimshaw's generalization that "the women found themselves caring for children and husbands and doing household chores rather than mission work." Both Wilcox and Lyman were teachers and Lucy continued Abner's "Select School" at Waioli, when her husband went to Boston for medical care of his son Albert; however, their large, young families required most of their time.

6. James W. Smith, M.D., November 14, 1855, Ms. Journal, Hawaiian Mission Children's Society. 31-32.

7. Damon, *Letters from the Life of Abner and Lucy Wilcox* 289-291; Thomas E. Armbruster, ed. *Smith Papers: The Letters and Journals of James William Smith and Melicent Knapp Smith, Medical Missionary Family in Koloa, Kauai, Hawaii* (San Marino High School: San Marino, California, 1999) 56.

8. O.A. Bushnell, *The Gifts of Civilization: Germs and Genocide in Hawaii* (University of Hawaii Press: Honolulu, 1993) 24, 289-290, 294-295. See also David Stannard, *Before the Horror: The Population of Hawaii on the Eve of Western Contact* (University of Hawaii Press: Honolulu, 1889) 3-146; Eleanor C. Nordyke, *The Peopling of Hawaii* (University of Hawaii Press: Honolulu, 1977) 14-20.

9. Barnes Riznik, *Waioili Mission House, Hanalei, Kauai* (Grove Farm Homestead and Waioli Mission House: Kauai, 1987) Statistical table, 1835-1863, p. 49; Armbruster, *Smith Papers*, 90.

10. Riznik, *Waioli Mission House*, 31

11. Damon, *Letters from the Life of Abner and Lucy Wilcox*, 291-292.

12. Armbruster, *Smith Papers,* 65-115. Chapter 3 "Vaccinating the Entire Island."

13. Bushnell, *The Gifts of Civilization,* 286.

14. Armbruster, *Smith Papers,* 56.

15. A recent history of efforts to eradicate smallpox disease worldwide, particularly the role of vaccination in treatment, can be found in Jonathan Tucker's *Scourge: The Once and Future Threat of Smallpox* (Atlantic Monthly Press: New York, 2001). The rise of America's hospitals is interpreted by Charles Rosenberg in *The Care of Strangers: The Rise of America's Hospital System* (Basic Books: New York, 1987) For hospitals in Hawaii, see Sumner Price, M.D. "Health Care in Hawaii," *Hospitals: Journal of the American Hospital Association,* 33, no. 10, May 16, 1959, 50-56.

16. Riznik, *Waioli Mission House,* pp. 37-49. The reform character of American Protestant missionary work has been discussed in many articles and books. For examples see Carl Kalani Beyer, "Manual and Industrial Education for Hawaiians During the 19th Century," *The Hawaiian Journal of History,* 38 (2004) 8-9, 17. Abner Wilcox's "Select School" at Waioli Mission Station and others introduced skills to their students "in order," as Beyer states, "to help Hawaians become self-sufficient, independent and economicallysuccessful." Other sources are also important: Lois Banner, "Religious Benevolence as Social Control: A Critique of An Interpretation," *Journal of American History,* 60 (June, 1973) 23-41; William R. Hutchison, *Errand to the World: American Protestant Thought and Foreirn Missions* (The University of Chicago Press: Chicago, 1987); John A. Andrew. III, *New England Congregationalists & Foreign Missions, 1800-1830* (University Press of Kentucky: Lexington, 1976).

Chapter Two: **Grove Farm**

1. Damon, *Letters from the Life of Abner and Lucy Wilcox,* 392-393.

2. Barnes Riznik, "Grove Farm Plantation History, 1864-1973," in O'Leary, *Register of the Grove Farm Plantation Records,* 7-17; Bob Krauss and William P. Alexander, *Grove Farm Plantation: The Biography of a Hawaiian Sugar Plantation* (Palo Alto: Pacific Books, 1965).

3. Mabel Wilcox, interview, January 8, 1973. Mabel I. Wilcox Papers, GFM.

4. Ibid.

5. Nancy O. Hedeman, *A Scottish Hawaiian Story: The Purvis Family in the Sandwich Islands* (Book Crafters: Virginia, 1994) 282-283.

6. James W. Smith, M. D., Ms. Journal, April 19, 1879. Kauai Museum.

7. Elsie H. Wilcox, typescript, "Early Race Relations on Kauai," n.d., Elsie H. Wilcox Papers, GFM.

8. M. Wilcox, interview, January 8, 1973.

9. Henry B. Townsend to Elsie Wilcox, August 28, 1936. Elsie H. Wilcox Papers, GFM.

10. Patricia W. Sheehan, "Emma Kauikeolani Napoleon Mahelona Wilcox," in Barbara B. Peterson, ed, *Notable Women of Hawaii* (University of Hawaii Press: Honolulu, 1984) 401-403; Rhoda E. A. Hackler and Maili Yardley, *The History of Kauikeolani Children's Hospital* (Kapiolani Health Care Foundation: Honolulu, 1994) 1-8, 52; Ethel M. Damon, *Koamalu: A Story of Pioneers on Kauai and of What They Built in the Garden Island* (Privately Printed: Honolulu, 1931) 2 vols,. II, 903-905; *The Story of Leahi: Fifty Years of Service* (Leahi Hospital: Honolulu, 1951) 5-15.

11. "Samuel W. Wilcox," in O'Leary, *Register of Grove Farm Plantation Records,* 22-23; *M. Wilcox,* interview, Janaury 8, 1973.

12. Krauss and Alexander, *Grove Farm Plantation,* 246-264.

13. Edward Joesting. *Kauai: The Separate Kingdom* (University of Hawaii Press and Kauai Museum Association: Honolulu, 1984) 252-259.

Chapter Three: **Mother and Daughter**

1. Sarah Lyman to Emma Wilcox, January 24, 1876 in Margaret Greer Martin, comp *Sarah Joiner Lyman of Hawaii: Her Own Story* (Lyman House Memorial Museum: Hilo, 1970) 160. Sarah wrote Emma of her feelings of attachment to her daughter a week after her wedding in Hilo to Samuel Wilcox, "You cannot know what

a trial it was for me to relinquish you to other hands."

2. S. Lyman to Lucia Hazen, April 13, 1877. Op. cit., 162.

3. Mabel Wilcox, interview, January 9, 1973.

4. Judith Dean Gething Hughes, *Women and Children First: The Life and Times of Elsie Wilcox of Kaua'i* (University of Hawaii Press: Honolulu, 1996) 28.

5. *Dana Hall, Graduation Excercises, Wednesday, June 19, 1901;* Ruth Woodman Russell, *Pine Manor: The First Fifty Years, 1911-1961* (Pine Manor Press: Pine Manor, 1969) 5. Helen Cooke was responsible for creating four distinct school units: Tenacre Country Day, Dana Hall Junior School, Dana Hall boarding and day school, and Pine Manor Junior College.

6. Russell, *Pine Manor,* 6.

7. Ibid. 15-16; *Dana Hall School Catalogue, 1901-l902,* 29-30; composition books, 1901. Mabel Wilcox Papers, GFM.

8. Etta Wilcox to Emma Wilcox, June 22, 1901. Samuel W. and Emma L. Wilcox Papers, GFM. Mabel wrote to her sister Etta on June 27, "Have you made all the arrangements for me next year? You better tell me what they are and what I have to do when I come back [from Europe]."

9. Quoted in Susan M. Reverby, *Ordered to Care: The Dilemma of American Nursing, 1850-1945* (Cambridge University Press: Cambridge, 1987) 15.

10. M. Wilcox to Emma Wilcox, September 24, 1901.

11. Gavan Daws, *Holy Man: Father Damien of Molokai* (Harper & Row: New York, 1973) 190-191, 209.

12. Dora Jane Isenberg Cole, "Mary Dorthea Rice Isenberg," in B. Paterson, *Notable Women of Hawaii,* 161-164; M. Wilcox, interview, January 9, 1973.

13. Ibid. M. Wilcox, interview.

14. Anna Scott Sloggett to author, April 9, 1995.

15. Hughes, *Women and Children First,* 33; Ms. diary-daybook, 1902. Elsie Hart Wilcox Papers, GFM.

16. Elsie Wilcox, diary-daybook, October 14, 1902.

17. Alice C. Wedemeyer, *The Story of the Mokihana Club of Kauai* (Privately printed: Kauai, 1987) 3-13.

18. "Richard John Wilkinson, In Memorium: Doctors of Hawaii," Hawaii Medical Library. Dr. Wilkinson received his medical education at Trinity College. After 1907 he returned to Ireland and England and engaged in private practice.; Hans Isenberg to F. L. Putman, November 17,1906. Lihue Plantation Collections, Hawaiian Sugar Planters' Association, Plantation Archives, Hamilton Library, University of Hawaii-Manoa; "Frank L. Putman, In Memorium: Doctors of Hawaii," Hawaii Medical Library. Mabel Wilcox's daybooks show that Putman was part of her Lihue Wilcox and Rice family social circle.

19. Chautauqua Correspondence School of Nursing, homestudy, M.Wilcox Papers, GFM.

Chapter Four: "A Model of Its Kind"

1. Mabel Wilcox, Formal Application, The Johns Hopkins Hospital School of Nurses, The Alan Chesney Medical Archives, The Johns Hopkins Medical Institutions. She was accepted in 1907 and entered the Preparatory Department on April 1, 1908; Ethel Johns and Blanche Pfefferkorn, *The Johns Hopkins Hospital School of Nursing, 1889-1949* (Baltimore: The Johns Hopkins Press, 1954) 120-183; for a general history see A. McGehee Harvey et. al. *A Model of Its Kind, Volume I: A Centennial History of Medicine at Johns Hopkins,* (The Johns Hopkins University Press: Baltimore, 1989).

2. M. Wilcox, interview, January 8, 1973; "James Robert Judd, In Memorium: Doctors of Hawaii," Hawaii Medical Library. The Episcopalian Bishop of Hawaii, Henry Restarick, also supported her application: "Applicant granddaughter of one of the old missionaries of Hawaiian people, and her family is one of the best known in Islands. By education and training she is a lady and in character a Christian woman above reproach. She is diligeant, able and of a quiet manner." Formal Application.

3. M.Wilcox, Diary-Daybook, 1908. Mabel I. Wilcox Papers, GFM.

4. Ibid.

5. Ibid.

6. Rosenberg, *The Care of Strangers, The Rise of America's Hospital System* (Basic Books: New York, 1987) 229, 232-238. If the course of study at Johns Hopkins Hospital was not an exception, Hopkins was among the first schools to reform the curriculum. As Rosenberg states, "An energetic and ambitious core of nursing superintendants, with the aid of like-thinking medical men, called for a recasting of nurse training, an improvement reflecting in attenuated form the parallel movement for reform in medical education."

7. Johns and Pfefferkorn, *The Johns Hopkins Hospital School of Nursing* 53.

8. Kenneth Ludmerer, M.D., *Learning to Heal: The Development of American Medical Education* (Basic Books: New York, 1985) 57.

9. M. Wilcox, Diary-Daybook, 1908. Her entries give a picture of the life of a student nurse and what Johns Hopkins Hospital training had to offer her. She passed her probationary work in July, 1908 and "entered the hospital."

10. M. Wilcox, Diary-Daybooks, 1908-1909. "Class history, senior division," *J.H.H.T.S.*, Commencement Number, vol.1, no.1 (May, 1911) 24-28. Mabel I. Wilcox Papers, GFM.

11. M. Wilcox, Diary-Daybook, 1909.

12. See Wilcox family tree in Krauss and Alexander, *Grove Farm Plantation,* Second Edition, 417-422.

13. M. Wilcox, Diary and Daybook, 1909.

14. Ibid. 1910.

15. Ibid.

16. *J.H.H.T.S.*, Commencement Number, 24-28.

17. M.Wilcox, Diary and Daybook, 1910.

18. *J.H.H.T.S.*, Commencement Number, 24-28.

19. Ibid. 4, 15-19. "Cerificate of Professional Training," Mabel I. Wilcox Papers, GFM. Her record of training in wards, operating rooms, and dispensaries showed 34 weeks in surgical wards, 32

weeks in general medical wards, 29 weeks in private patients, 12 weeks in gynecological wards, 10 weeks in operating rooms, nine weeks in obstetrical wards, and 18 weeks of night duty.

20. Johns and Pfeffercorn, *The Johns Hopkins School of Nursing,* 170-183.

21. *J.H.H.T.S.,* Commencement Number, 40-43.

22. Quantitative analysis of 1911 class compiled from the indexed records of *The Johns Hopkins Nurses Alumnae Magazine* in the Alan Chesney Medical Archives.

23. Reverby, *Ordered to Care,* p. 158

Chapter Five: Wilikoki: Kauka Wahine

1. Hughes, *Women and Children First,* 50-53; Wedemeyer, *The Story of the Mokihana Club of Kauai,* 20-24. Mabel began her year as club president in October, 1914. Wedemeyer writes, "..under the leadership of Miss Mabel Wilcox, the club turned attention to matters concerning public health and public health nursing.

2. Krauss and Alexander, *Grove Farm Plantation,* 301-303; Hughes, *Women and Children First,* ibid.

3. Archibald N. Sinclair, M.D. to Mabel Wilcox, October 31, 1913. Mabel I. Wilcox Papers, GFM; John Duffy, *The Sanitarians: A History of American Public Health* (University of Illinois Press, Urbana, 1990) 197-201. Dr. Sinclair was Territorial Board of Health Superintendant of the Anti-Tuberculosis Bureau.

4. A.N. Sinclair, "Tuberculosis Pulmonalis," *Transactions of the Thirteenth Annual Meeting of the Hawaiian Medical Society...*(Honolulu, 1905), 43; *The Garden Island,* September 19, October 12, November 12 and December 10, 1912. The newspaper articles are examples of the public education work of the Anti-Tuberculosis Bureau.

5. A. Sinclair to M. Wilcox, October 31, 1913.

6. *The Sunday Star-Bulletin and Advertiser,* October 31, 1965.

7. Mabel Wilcox, Ms. Mokihana Club talk, 1916. Mabel I Wilcox Papers, GFM.

8. Ibid.

9. Mark Caldwell, *The Last Crusade: The War on Consumption* (Atheneum: New York, 1988) 4-9.

10. *Honolulu Advertiser,* February 20, 27, 1912; July 17, 1917.

11. Rene Dubois, *Mirage of Health: Utopias, Progress, and Biological Change* (Anchor Books: Garden City, 1959), 160-163.

12. M. Wilcox, Mokihana Club talk, 1916; Margaret M. L. Catton, *Social Service in Hawaii* (Pacific Books: Palo Alto, 1959) 104.

13. *The Sunday Star- Bulletin and Advertiser.* October 31, 1965. The correspondence files of the Department of Health, State Archives contain a letter from Dr. Frank Putman in which he wrote on July 4, 1911: I had a conversation this morning with Mr. Geo. Wilcox regarding tuberculosis work on Kauai. He seemed very favorably inclined toward helping along with the work and we discussed the advisability of creating a settlement of cottages with nurses and attendants to work in conjunction with the district nurses of the whole island. There was nothing definite developed but I believe he would be glad to place some of his more than abundant resources at our disposal if the question were gone at in the right way.

14. M. Wilcox, Mokihana Club talk, 1916.

15. Peter Kim, M.D. , "History of Samuel Mahelona Memorial Hospital," typescript, 1952. *passim.* Mabel I. Wilcox Papers; Peter Kim, interview, April 23, May 14, 1982. GFM.

16. M. Wilcox, Mokihana Club talk, 1916; *The Garden Island,* July 24, 1917.

17. Charles O. Uhlmann, "Clinton Briggs Ripley--Architect: The Middle Years," *Hawaii Architect,* 8, no.2 (February, 1979) 12-19; Caldwell, *The Last Crusade,* 87-97, for general discussion of sanatoria plans and routines.

Chapter Six: **Kauai's Mothers and Children**

1. Gabriel I, interview, June 22, 1982. Mabel I. Wilcox Papers, GFM.

2. M. Wilcox , Mokihana Club talk, 1916, Mabel I Wilcox Papers, GFM.

3. Eleanor C. Nordyke, *The Peopling of Hawaii,* (University of Hawaii Press: Honululu, 1989) Second Edition, 238, Table 4-7.

4. Nordyke, *The Peopling of Hawaii*, 102, Figure 4-3;109-112, Tables 4-5, 4-6.

5. Betty Sora, R.N., interview, February 16, 1982. GFM.

6. Alice Young Kohler, Ph.N, interview. and papers, August 6, 1985. GFM; Susan L. Smith, "Medicine, Midwifery and the State: Japanese Americans and Health Care in Hawaii, 1885-1945," *JAAS* (February, 2001) 57-75.

7. James Rath to Mabel Wilcox, July 3, 1917. Mokihana Club Papers, Kauai Museum; Wedemeyer, *The Story of the Mokihana Club*, 125-131; Fanny Kuhling, R.N. to Mabel Wilcox, July 8, 11, 1917, Mokihana Club Papers, Kauai Museum.

8. Catton, *Social Service in Hawaii,* 42, 147; Richard A. Meckel, *Save the Babies: American Public Health Reform and the Prevention of Infant Mortality, 1850-1929,* (The Johns Hopkins University Press: Baltimore, 1990), 129. Meckel states that " by 1915 hundreds of private agencies in almost 300 American cities and towns were conducting some form of educational infant welfare work." Palama Settlement, the Mokihana Club and the Alexander Settlement on Mauai are examples of such nursing services, Margaret M.L. Catton, *Social Service in Hawaii* (Pacific Books: Palo Alto, 1959) 42, 147

9. Wedemeyer, *The Story of the Mokihana Club,* 126-127.

10. M. Wilcox, Mokihana Club talk, 1916. GFM.

11. M. Wilcox, recruiting letter, July 9, 1917. Mokihana Club Papers, Kauai Museum.

12. M. Wilcox, minutes of Nurses Committee, May 29, 1920, Mokihana Club Papers, Kauai Museum.

13. Sarah Cheek, R.N., "Report from December 19 to June, 1920," Mokihana Club Papers, Kauai Museum.

14. Vera Marston, R.N., "Report from May, 1921 to June, 1922," Mokihana Club Papers, Kauai Museum.

15. Barnes Riznik, "From Barracks to Family Homes: A Social History of Labor Housing Reform on Hawaii's Sugar Plantations," *The Hawaiian Journal of History,* 33 (1999), 119-157.

16. Ibid. 133-134.

17. Meckel, *Save the Babies,* 1.

Chapter Seven: War Nurse

1. Besse Baker to Mabel Wilcox, n.d. Mabel I. Wilcox Papers, GFM.

2. M. Wilcox, interview, January 8, 1973. GFM.

3. M. Wilcox to Emma Wilcox, November 25, 1917. Samuel W. and Emma L. Wilcox Papers, GFM. Ethel Damon enlisted in the canteen service of the American Red Cross. Her missionary family on Oahu were long-time friends of the Wilcoxes. She had been teaching French and German at Punahou School.

4. For two accounts of the Red Cross Children's Bureau in France written directly after World War I, see Sarah Pickett, "Nursing Service to the Civilian Population," in Lavina Dock, et. al., *History of American Red Cross Nursing,* (Macmillan: New York, 1922) 756-982 and John van Schaick, Jr., *The Little Corner Never Conquered: The Story of the American Red Cross War Work in Belgium,* (Macmillan: New York, 1922), 177-183. The following interpretive studies of infant welfare, the French nation's depopulation crisis, and the role of the Red Cross in World War I are important: Meckel, *Save the Babies:* Alisa Klaus, *Every Child a Lion: The Origins of Maternal and Infant Health Policy in the United States and France, 1890-1920),* (Cornell University Press: Ithaca, 1993); and Joseph J. Spenger, *France Faces Depopulation,* (Duke University Press: Durham, 1976) 121-134.

5. M.Wilcox to Emma Wilcox, December 4, 1917, GFM; M. Wilcox, Diary-Daybook, 1917, GFM; M. Wilcox, transcript, "Personal Report of Service in the Red Cross," 1919, GFM; Helen B. Taussig, "Edwards A. Park, 1878-1969," *Journal of Pediatrics,* 77, No.4 (October, 1970) 722-731. Before sailing from New York City, Mabel Wilcox wrote her mother: "My outfit is for a Red Cross Hospital not a Military Hospital. I didn't get a sleeping

bag or poncho or rubber boots, so I'm evidently to be indoors. I have my sealed orders in my suitcase now & tell you I'm mighty curious about that envelope."

6. M. Wilcox, Diary-Daybook, 1917-1918. GFM.

7. Ibid.

8. "James R. Judd," Hawaii Medical Library.

9. M. Wilcox to " family," December 30, 1917. GFM.

10. M. Wilcox to " folks at home," December 23, 1917. GFM.

11. M. Wilcox, Diary-Daybook, 1917-1918; M. Wilcox to "folks at home," January 6, 1918. GFM.

Chapter Eight: "A Perfect Medical Unit"

1. M. Wilcox to "family," December 30, 1917. GFM.

2. Pickett, "Nursing Service to the Civilian Population," in Dock, *History of Red Cross Nursing*, 756-982; Edwards A. Park, M.D. et. al. "A Children's Dispensary Organized on the Basis of Appointments for Patients," *The Modern Hospital,* 13 (August, 1919) 101-108; see also Park, "Un Dispensaire De La Croix-Rouge Americaine En France," *Archives de Medicine des Enfants,* 1919, XXII (no 8). Mabel Wilcox and Ethel Damon contributed to the article and reports, Damon providing the translation.

3. M. Wilcox, Mokihana Club talk, 1919. GFM; Wedemeyer, *The Story of the Mokihana Club*, 32-33.

4. Ibid.

5. M. Wilcox to "family," Janauary 20, 1918. GFM.

6. M. Wilcox, Mokihana Club talk, 1919. GFM.

7. Pickett, "Nursing Service to the Civilian Population," 231, 242, 530; M. Wilcox, Diary-Daybook, 1917-1918.

8. Taussig, "Edwards A. Park," 724.

9. M. Wilcox to "family," January 20, 1918. M. Wilcox to Emma Wilcox, March 3, 1918. GFM.

10. Ethel Damon to Mrs. H. B. Gifford, April 7, 1918. GFM. Several of Damon's accounts of Paris and Le Havre were later printed in Honolulu newspapers.

11. M. Wilcox to Emma Wilcox, March 3, 1918. GFM.

12. M. Wilcox, Diary-Daybook, 1917-1918. GFM. Van Schaick, Park and Wilcox met February 5 and 7. Park "recommended that they withdraw."

13. M. Wilcox to Emma Wilcox, March 3, 1918. GFM.

14. Ibid.

15. M. Wilcox, Diary-Daybook, 1917-1918. GFM.

16. Ibid.

17. Ibid.

18. M. Wilcox to Emma Wilcox, April 25, 1918. GFM.

19. M. Wilcox, Mokihana Club talk, 1919.

20. M. Wilcox, Diary-Daybook, 1917-1918. GFM; Park, "A Children's Dispensary Organized on the Basis of Appointments," 186-187; Van Schaick, *The Little Corner Never Conquered*, 180-181. In a chapter, "Dr. Park's Great Experiment," van Schaick commended Dr. Park: "scientific. accurate, precise. careful to a degree though he is, nobody could enter an institution run by Dr. Park without feeling a deep genuine and all pervading human sympathy." Van Schaick acknowledged that "there were local jealousies and divisions on the way..."

21. Park, "A Children's Dispensary," 105.

22. Taussig, "Edwards Park" 724.

23. M. Wilcox to Emma Wilcox, July 10, 1918. GFM. Another of Mabel Wilcox's contributions was the organization of a training course for nurses' aids. Her papers include the course outline with its emphasis on infant and child care and dietetics. She wrote, "These aids have had in three months as thorough a course in the nursing of sick children as it is possible to give them."

24. Ibid.

25. Mabel Wilcox, Diary-Daybook, 1917-1918. GFM.

26. M. Wilcox to Emma Wilcox, July 10, 1918, GFM.

27. Taussig, "Edwards A. Park," 726; A. Harvey Mc.Ghee et. al. *A Model of Its Kind, Volume I,* 56, 74, 213, 279.

28. M. Wilcox, Mokihana Club talk, 1919. GFM.

29. M. Wilcox, Diary-Daybook, 1917-1918.

30. Ibid.

31. M. Wilcox, Mokihana Club talk, 1919. GFM.

32. E. Damon, Red Cross final report, "Six Months of Dispensary Work at Salle Franklin," Mabel I. Wilcox Papers. GFM. Damon wrote, "It is felt that a definite scientific beginning has been made against infant mortaility, and negotiations are now pending for the transfer of the entire work from the Red Cross to the French municipal and departmental authorities." Taussig later wrote, "By means of this combination of a perfect little hospital, the children...received the best that American medicine could offer." Klaus in *Every Child a Lion,* 266-269, offers historical perspective on the complex relationship of politics, religion and the birthrate in France after World War I.

33. Van Schaick, *The Little Corner Never Conquered,* 181-183.

34. I wish to acknowledge the assistance of the Hawaii Medical Library in obtaining copies of these articles.

35. M. Wilcox, Mokihana Club talk, 1919.

36. Meckel, *Save the Babies,* 201.

37. M. Wilcox to Elsie Wilcox, April 15, 1919. GFM; Wedemeyer, *The Story of the Mokihana Club,* 136.

38. M. Wilcox to Elsie Wilcox, July 19, September 5, and September 21, 1919. GFM

Chapter Nine: **Public Health in Everyday Life on Kauai**

1. M. Wilcox, Mokihana Club talk, 1919. GFM; Charles Katsumu Tanimoto, *Return to Mahaulepu: Personal Sketches* (Fisher Printing Co.: Honolulu, 1982) 173. Tanimoto added that "Two years later,

I saw my angel again. This time she came with her elder sister, Elsie. They were the trustees of the dormitory where I resided as a high school student."

2. Hughes, *Women and Children First*, 72-73.

3. Ms. Minutebook, March, 1921-December, 1949. Board of Trustees, Samuel Mahelona Hospital, pp. 5-7. Samuel Mahelona Memorial Hospital; Hughes, *Women and Children First,* 58-70. Mabel Wilcox served as the treasurer, 1919-1957.

4. Riznik, *Waioli Mission House,* 66; Wedemeyer, *The Story of the Mokihana Club,* 120-121, 210.

5. Krauss and Alexander, *Grove Farm Plantation,* 312-313, 337.

6. Riznik, *Waioli Mission House,* 64, 78, 81; Ethel Damon to George N. Wilcox, July 9. 1920. George N. Wilcox Papers. GFM; she had written to G.N. Wilcox earlier. "Even before the work of the Centennial brought up various things worth doing---such as a new edition of Obookiah's memoirs---I had planned. on my return from France, to put all my time on the study of Hawaiian literature and history."

7. Peter Kim, interview, April 23, May 14, 1982. GFM.

8. Lawrence Ferreiro, interview, March 26, 1985. GFM.

9. Ibid.

10. Miyoko Ednaco, interview, June 6, 1982, October 6, 1987. GFM.

11. It is clear that Kauai's physicians needed to be led into aggressive referrals of persons infected with tuberculosis to Mahelona.

12. Ms. Minutebook, Samuel Mahelona Memorial Hospital, 39-42; Series 259, Ms. Minutes of the Board of Health, 1858-1983, vol. 24, July 8, 1925-June 30, 1927. Hawaii State Archives. The minutes of December 16, 1925 reported that "Three tuberculosis clinics are being conducted on that island with the assistance of Dr. Duryea, the Superintendent of Samuel Mahelona Hospital, and the Public Health Nurses of the Board of Health in getting in the cases. Chest clinics are also being conducted for underweight and undernourished children...It is very encouraging to notice the good feeling and spirit of cooperation."

13. Ms. Minutebook, Samuel Mahelona Memorial Hospital, 56-83; *The Honolulu Advertiser,* April 30, 1926.

14. Ms. Minutes of the Board of Health, October 21, 1925. Mabel Wilcox was appointed Nurse, Division of Maternity and Infancy, Kauai, September 1,1925; M. Smyth, "Public Health Nursing in Hawaii," *The Pacific Coast Journal of Nursing,"* 298; M. Smyth, "What is a Public Health Nurse?", *First Territorial Conference of Social Work* (Honolulu, April 23-29, 1921). Smyth described the exisiting program at Palama Settlement in Honolulu prior to the passage of the federal Sheppard-Towner Maternity and Infant Act in 1921. For an overview of the Sheppard-Towner program nationally, see Meckel, *Save the Babies,* Chapter 8 , "Defeat in Victory, Victory in Defeat: The Sheppard-Towner Act." In February, 1927 the General Meeting of the Mokihana Club endorsed the Board of Health's operation of the new health centers. See Wedemeyer, *The Story of the Mokihana Club,* 147.

15. "Vivia Belle Appleton, In Memorium, Doctors of Hawaii," Hawaii Medical Library. At the program of the 1921 First Territorial Conference of Public Work, Appleton said, "With regard to our immigrants, the standard of cleanliness among our immigrants here is much higher than it is in the States, but the standard of diet is not so...The racial diets here are not satisfactory." Appleton was reflecting an approach to public health practice and research influenced by her Johns Hopkins Medical School training in the new field of pediatrics, her hospital internships, work with William P. Lucas, and her wartime experiences with the Children's Bureau in France.

16. V. B. Appleton, "Report of the Division of Maternal and Infant Hygiene," *Annual Report of the President of the Board of Health of the Territory of Hawaii of the Fiscal Year Ending June 20, 1926* (Honolulu, 1927).

17. *Honolulu Star Bulletin*, April 15, 1927.

18. Vera Marston, Ms. Report from May 1, 1921 to June, 1922, Mokihana Club Papers. Kauai Museum.

19. Hughes, *Woman and Children First,* 87-88.

20. Ibid.

21. Josephina Cortezan, interview, January 29, 1982. GFM.

22. V. B. Appleton, "Report of the Division of Maternal and Infant Hygiene," 1926.

23. V. B. Appleton, "Report of the Division of Maternal and Infant Hygiene." 1927.

24. Umeyo Tamashiro, interview, June 3, 1986. GFM.

25. Harry S. Mustard, *Rural Health Practice* (Commonwealth Fund: New York, 1936) 258-299; Meckel, *Save the Babies*, p. 212.

26. Edith Nicholson, interview,

27. V.B. Appleton, "Report of the Division of Maternal and Infant Hygiene," 1927.

28. M. Smyth, "Public Health Nursing in Hawaii," *The Pacific Coast Journal of Nursing.* p. 298.

29. E. Fee, *Disease & Discovery* p.18, 20-22, 122-130. Fee discusses the diversity of professional public health views of the time, from infectious disease control to broader conceptions of disease prevention and health promotion. Mabel Wilcox's nursing and medical library at Grove Farm represents such diversity. She continued to add to her office library in the cottage at Grove Farm. Books by such leaders in the "new public health". Charles-Edward A. Winslow, Elmer V. McCollum, Milton Rosenau, William R. P. Emerson and William P. Lucas can be found there with the earlier works on sanitation and disease control.

Chapter Ten: Collaboration and Conflict

1. Diane Kaplan et. al., "Ira Vaughn Hiscock Papers, Manuscript Group Number 1284, Sterling Memorial Library Contemporary Medical Care and Health Policy Collection," Yale University. Archival finding aid, 1982, pp. 1-16; Ira V. Hiscock, *A Survey of Health and Welfare Activities in Honolulu, Hawaii,* Committee on Administrative Practice, American Public Health Association (Quinnipiack Press: New Haven, 1929) 5-160. Karen Buhler-Wilkerson, "False Dawn: The Rise and Decline of Public Health

Nursing in America, 1900-1930," in Lagemann, ed. *Nursing History: New Perspectives, New Possibilities,* 89-101.

2. V. B. Appleton, *First Territorial Conference of Social Work.*

3. *Transactions of the Thirty-Fourth Annual Meeting of the Hawaii Territorial Medical Society* (Honolulu, 1924).

4. *Transactions of the Thirty-Seventh Annual Meeting of the Hawaii Territorial Medical Society* (Honolulu, 1927).

5. Paul Starr, *The Social Transformation of American Medicine* (Basic Books: New York, 1982) 181 ff.

6. Margaret M. L. Catton, *Social Service in Hawaii,* (Pacific Books, Palo Alto, 1959) 42-49; "Margaret Bergen: A Sketch of Tribute," *Honolulu Advertiser,* July 24, 1938. To help create a better understanding of problems of malnutrition, in 1922 Bergin arranged to have William R. P. Emerson of the Nutrition Clinics for Delicate Children in Boston conduct a course in Honolulu for nurses, teachers and social workers.

7. *Annual Report of the Board of Health, 1926.*

8. Ms. Minutes of the Board of Health, February 17, March 17, 1926. Hawaii State Archives.

9. "Frederick Eugene Trotter. In Memorium: Doctors of Hawaii," Hawaii Medical Library.

10. Ms. Minutes of the Board of Health, November 19, December 15, 1926.

11. Ms. Minutes of the Board of Health, May 18, June 9, 1927.

12. Ms. Minutes of the Board of Health, July 20, 1927, vol. 25, July 20, 1927- December 19, 1928.

13. Ms. Minutes of the Board of Health, July 26, 1927.

14. Ethel M. Damon, "Mabel Leilani Smyth," *Hawaii Medical Journal and Inter-island Nurses' Bulletin,* vol. 16, no. 5 (May-June, 1957) 560-562; M. Smyth to M. Wilcox, August 3, 1927. GFM. Mabel Wilcox's papers include an extensive incoming correspondence from Mabel Smyth, 1927 to 1937. The letters are significant especially because the State of Hawaii Department of Health,

according to former State Archivist Agnes Conrad, did not later retain any of the bureau records from Kauai.

15. *Annual Report of the Board of Health, 1928.*

16. M. Smyth to M. Wilcox, n.d. GFM.

17. Annual Report of the Board of Health, 1929.

18. Ibid.

19. *Annual Report of the Board of Health, 1930.* As a Hawaiian, Smyth was personally knowlegeable. "The Hawaiian mother does not avail herself of health facilities offered as readily as some of our other racial groups," she wrote.

20. M. Bergen to M. Wilcox, December 10, 1930. GFM.

21. Smyth wrote in her annual report, "This survey marks a new era in the development of public health activities, not only in Honolulu, but throughout the whole Territory, for what standards are set here, permeate throughout the whole Territorial organization." Smyth repeatedly asked that a full-time physician be appointed to direct her Division of Maternal and Infant Hygiene. Richard K.C. Lee cited the importance of Hiscock's 1929 survey and Hiscock's follow-up work in 1935 and 1950 in "Public Health Contrasts in Hawaii, 1850-1953," Reports, 408-409. Lee received his public health doctorate in 1938 from Yale and studied with Hiscock. Lee joined the Teritorial Department of Public Health and became its Director in 1943.

Chapter Eleven: From Dream to Reality

1. Scrapbook, 1929-1949, Kauai Tuberculosis Association. Mabel Wilcox Papers. GFM.

2. G. N. Wilcox to M. Wilcox, April 7, 1931. G. N. Wilcox Papers. GFM.

3. G. N. Wilcox, interviews, 1921-1932. GFM.

4. *Honolulu Star-Bulletin,* May 18, 1936; Kauai Tuberculosis Scrapbook.

5. Ira V. Hiscock, "Report of the Brief Study of Public Health Work," September 6, 1935." Typescript, Mabel Wilcox Papers. GFM; Bruce H. Douglas, *Tuberculosis in the Territory of Hawaii* (n.p.: Honolulu, 1938) 41-45.

6. Ethel Damon, *Koamalu,* II, 902-904.

7. Nils P. Larsen, "A Field Portrait of Dr. J. Kuhns in Action," *The Queen's Hospital Bulletin,* vol. 6, no. 2 (July, 1929); Robert Worth, comments, November, 21, 1988, public forum transcript, "Perspectives on Health Care and Healing on Kauai: 200 Years of Change" GFM.

8. Marvin Brennecke, interview, April 16, 1982. GFM.

9. Kay Irwin, interview, April 11, 1980. Kauai Museum.

10. M. Brennecke, interview, April 16, 1982. GFM.

11. Annual Report, Lihue Hospital, 1919, 1930. Typescripts. Mabel Wilcox Papers. GFM.

12. Ira V. Hiscock, "Health Work on a Sugar Plantation," *American Journal of Public Health,* vol.26, no. 9 (1936). He described the advances in plantation medicine and public health care at Waialua Agricultural Company on Oahu; *Report on Industrial Relations in the Hawaiian Sugar Industry Prepared for the Hawaiian Sugar Planters' Association,* (Curtis, Fosdick & Belknap: New York, 1926) II, 214-215. GFM; Robert Worth, comments, November 21, 1988. GFM; Tsugie Kadota, a longtime Wilcox Hospital nurse, provided another important perspective on plantation medicine.

13. Nils Larsen to Anna Williams, July 5, 1939. Mabel Wilcox Papers. GFM; See also Helen Wong Smith, "Nils P. Larsen, M. D., and Plantation Medicine," a public lecture delivered at Wilcox Hospital, January 10, 1999. Typescript, GFM / The paper provides a summary of Larsen's health care views and his articles about plantation medicine. Robert Worth's perspective on plantation is also valuable: "The whole plantation system was very different...they made their people very dependent on medical help available, because for a long time people used to come to the (plantation) clinic for every little ailment...because it

was offered free to them and that was what they were told to do."
Interview, February 26, 1982. GFM.

14. Robert Worth, interview, May 16, 1982. GFM.

15. Ibid.

16. Ibid.

17. See Rosemary Stevens' discussion of hospital standardization, *In Sickness and in Wealth,* 114-120; Larsen, "Hospital Standardization," *Plantation Health Bulletin,* vol.1, no. 2 (October, 1936).

18. Mabel Wilcox continued to add to her office library at Grove Farm. New titles about hospitals included Frank Chapman, *Hospital Organization and Operation;* Michael Davis, *Clinics, Hospitals and Health Centers;* Malcolm T. Mac Eachern, *Hospital Organization and Management;* Warren Morrill, *The Hospital Manual of Operations; and* Rufus Rorem, *The Public's Investment in Hospitals;*

19. M. Wilcox, "Proposal for the Operation of Lihue Hospital," typescript, 1930; Board of Health Hospital and Clinic Service Planning and Survey notes, 1934-1936. Mabel Wilcox Papers, GFM; The minutes kept by the Kauai Nurses Association show that some of the topics of its speakers parallel those of the HSPA's programs for plantation physicians. Mabel Wilcox Papers. GFM.

20. M. Wilcox, "Proposal for the Operation of the Lihue Hospital."

21. Richard K. C. Lee, interview, June 3, 1982. GFM.

22. M. Wilcox, "Proposal for the Operation of the Lihue Hospital."

23. Griffin, *Wilcox Memorial,* 3-4; Barnes Riznik, "The Origins of Wilcox Hospital" in Ruth Smith, ed. *Perspective on Health Care and Healing on Kauai: 200 Years of Change: Introduction to the Exhibition and Public Forums, Kauai Museum, October 26, 1988 through Janauary 25, 1989.* (Lihue: Kauai Musuem, 1988). Sixteen-page tabloid, 7-10.

Chapter Twelve: **Retirement from Territorial Nursing**

1. Krauss and Alexander, *Grove Farm Plantation,* Second Edition, "The Wilcox Family," 417-422.

2. Riznik, *Waioli Mission House,* 79.

3. *Honolulu Star-Bulletin,* May 26, 1937.

4. Hiscock, "Health Work on a Sugar Plantation in Hawaii."

5. Smyth, "Public Health Nursing in Hawaii."

6. *Honolulu Star-Bulletin,* February 2, 1935. M. Wilcox to Helen Lyman, February 8-April 15, 1935. Mabel Wilcox Papers. GFM.

7. Mabel Wilcox hospital notes, September, 1935. Mabel Wilcox Papers. GFM.

8. N. Larsen to M. Wilcox, September 21, 1935. Mabel Wilcox Papers. GFM.

9. Riznik, "The Origins of Wilcox Hospital."

10. Elizabeth H. Middleton, "History of G. N. Wilcox Memorial Hospital, 1938-1963." Typescript. Mabel Wilcox Papers. GFM. Lindsay Faye to Elsie Wilcox, August 14, 1935. Elsie Wilcox Papers. GFM. *The Garden Island,* January, 22, 1929 carried a detailed description of the layout of the new hospital in Waimea.

11. Burt Wade, interview, March 19, 1982. GFM.

12. Griffin, *Wilcox Memorial Hospital,* 3-4.

13. Dickey's plans for the nurses' residence in 1937 showed ten two-person rooms, but Thomas Perkins planned single rooms in a progressive garden quadrangle complex. Perkins was in the Honolulu office of Claude A. Stiehl, and he sometimes also worked for Dickey. Perkins was assisted by Alan Faye who designed the new Grove Farm Co. office at Puhi. Grove Farm constructed the "Four Courts" with concrete hollow tiles it made in Puhi.

14. Hanna Hotvedt interview, June, 1977. GFM.

Chapter Thirteen: On Governing Boards

1. Riznik, "The Origins of Wilcox Hospital" ; Rosenberg, *The Care of Strangers,* 348.

2. Griffin, *Wilcox Memorial Hospital,* 13.

3. Elizabeth Middleton, interview, February 12, February 19, 1982. GFM.

4. Ibid.

5. Tsugie Kadota, interview, February 26, March 12, 1982; April 2, 1998. GFM. Kadota, a graduate of Queen's Hospital Nurses' School in 1942, was on the Wilcox Hospital staff for over 40 years. Her recollections of Middleton are significant and she said, "She was always on top of things. She came to us with a wealth of information, and she was an example for us to follow. She was all over the place working herself. " Kadota also said that at the nurses' residence Middleton was a completely different person: "We were all equal then, she was no longer our boss so we did a lot of card games together, and she used to get a group together and put on plays."

6. Griffin, *Wilcox Memorial Hospital,* 8.

7. A. Mooklar to author, October 15, 1982.

8. Griffin, *Wilcox Memorial Hospital,* 21.

9. P. Coke to Pat Griffin, April 17, 2000.

10. *The Annual Report of the Samuel Mahelona Memorial Hospital for the Fiscal Year Ending June 30, 1953;* Kim, "History of Samuel Mahelona Memorial Hospital."

11. R. Worth, interview, May 6, 1982. GFM.

12. Evelyn Mott-Smith, interview, April 27, 1982. GFM. Mott-Smith recalled, "As we left for the trip Miss Elsie gave me a big, fat envelope. Full of greenbacks!" She said, "Miss Mabel is kind of close, you know, and this is what I'd call your cushion. I want you, anyplace you are to take her out to any theaters there are--anything that's fun--anyplace to go that's fun while you are on the trip.' "

Chapter Fourteen: A Dual Legacy: Preserving Grove Farm

1. Holbrook Goodale to author, April 18, 2002; Riznik, "Shopping for New England Antiques and Collecting Family Heirlooms in the Restoration of Hawaii's Waioli Mission House," paper delivered at the Dublin Seminar for New England Folklife: New

England Collectors and Collections, June 19, 2004. There are number of studies analyzing motivations of American women as cultural custodians. Helpful works are Gail Lee Dubrow & Jennifer Goodman, eds., *Restoring Women's History through Historic Preservation* (Johns Hopkins University Press: Baltimore, 2003) Parts I and II; Patricia West, *Domesticating America's House Museums* (Smithsonian Institution Press: Washington, 1999); Kathleen D. Mc Carthy, *Women's Culture: American Philanthropy and Art, 1830-1930* (University of Chicago Press: Chicago, 1991; and Michael Kammen, *Mystic Chords of Memory: The Tranformation of Tradition in American Culture* (Vintage Books: New York, 1991) 266-271.

2. Riznik, *Waioli Mission House,* 81-82.

3. Ibid.

4. William Brigham to Samuel Wilcox, March 26, 1900. Samuel W. and Emma L. Wilcox Papers, GFM; *List of Accessions, Director's Annual Report for 1911.* The report gives a picture of the Bishop Museum's collecting and museum loans from Kauai. John F. G. Stokes, the Bishop Museum's anthropologist examined Samuel Wilcox's collection of Hawaiian artifacts at Grove Farm in 1913; Damon, *Letters from the Life of Abner and Lucy Wilcox;* E. Wilcox, *A Record of the Descendants of Abner Wilcox and Lucy Eliza Hart Wilcox, 1836- 1950* (Privately Printed: Honolulu, 1950).

5. Damon, *Samuel Chenery Damon* (Hawaiian Mission Children's Society: Honolulu, 1966).

6. Samuel Cooke to author, April 20, 2002; Robert Schleck, "Notes of Miss Mabel's Hawaiiana Collection," typescript, 1995. GFM; M. Wilcox to Thelma Hadley, August 19, 1969, Wilcox Library file. GFM.

7. G. N. Wilcox interviews. GFM.

8. Gavan Daws to author, February 17, 2002.

9. R. Schleck to author, April 1, 2002.

10. Sophie Cluff to William Atkins, April 27, 1990; "Obituary notes" by Debbie Hayward and Elizabeth Judd, April 27, 1996. Sophie Judd Cluff files. GFM.

11. R. Schleck to author, April 1, 2002.

12. R. Schleck, "Reminiscences of MIW," typescript, June 2, 2002. GFM.

13. "Notes of a Discussion by Mabel I. Wilcox with James Hunt, Director, Hawaii State Library; Janet Bell, Sinclair Library, University of Hawaii; Thelma Hadley, Kauai Public Library; and S. Cluff concerning Wilcox Library," May 17, 1968. Wilcox Library file. GFM.

14. Kauai Regional Library, "Elsie H. Wilcox and Mabel I. Wilcox Collection," 1978; Carol White to Board of Directors, Waioli Corporation, May 15, 1995. Wilcox Library file. GFM. Explaining reasons for the return of the collection White wrote, "The financial outlook for libraries is bleak. Because of current and projected budget shortfalls, we are forced to relocate the Bookmobile collection into Lihue Library's shelf space. Further, we have suffered a net loss of two employees in the last 3 months, whom we cannot replace because of the current hiring freeze. Because of these severe space and staff constrictions, we are no longer able to properly maintain the Collection."

15. S. Cluff to W. Atkins, April 27, 1990.

16. Robert Bromberg to author, August 5, 2002.

17. Kammen, *Mystic Chords of Memory,* 635.

18. Pamela Wilcox Dohrman to author, n.d., 2002. Edward Beechert to author, August 30, 2002.

19. Mary Jane Knight, "Celebrating 25 Years of Service to Hawaii's Museum Community," HMA Directory, 1993.

20. "Notes by George Moore re Grove Farm Museum," typescript, August 25, 1968. GFM; the Grove Farm Museum Committee was formed in January, 1969. Family members of the committee were Mabel Wilcox, Richard Sloggett, Sam Wilcox, Nancy Goodale, Patsy Sheehan and Gale Carswell, along with Sophie Cluff.

21. Frank Broadbent to Richard Sloggett, February 4, 1969; W. M. Moragne, December 27, 1968. Grove Farm Museum file. GFM.

22. S. Cluff to Geoffrey Fairfax, October 19, 1971. Grove Farm Museum file. GFM; Edith K. Wilcox to author, Janaury 27, 2002.

23. M. Wilcox to Chairman and Members, Planning Commission, County of Kauai, November 15, 1971, with attachment. Grove Farm Museum file. GFM.

24. Sophie Cluff to Jane Silverman, November 9, 1972. Private Collection.

25. Ibid.

26. Schleck, "Reminiscences of MIW."

27. Ibid.

28. Ibid.

29. S. Cluff to J. Silverman, December 6, December 27, 1972; B. Riznik to J. Silverman, December 4, 1972. Private Collection.

30. Discussion of Grove Farm Museum plans by M. Wilcox, S. Cluff and B. Riznik, typescript, January 6, 1973. Grove Farm Museum file. GFM.

31. Ibid.

32. Ibid.

33. Ibid.

34. Ibid.

35. Ibid.

36. Schleck to author, April 1, 2002.

37. S. Cluff to J. Silverman, January 25, 1973. Private Collection.

38. Kathryn Hulme, "They Called Her Wilikoki," typescript, December 18, 1975. Yale University Library; Anne C. May, "The Kathryn Hulme Collection," *The Yale Library Gazette,* vol. 53, no. 3 (January, 1976), 129-134. Hulme, the author of *The Nun's Story,* lived on Kauai and began a biography of Mabel Wilcox but completed only one chapter. During her research she asked Mabel Wilcox why she had never married. Hulme wrote, "A very lovely old lady in her well-preserved late eighties was looking at me. She tossed her immaculately combed white hair and said with a faint hint of defiance: 'I was having a good time, wasn't I?'"

39. A list of the Board of Trustees and Officers from 1974 to 1989 can be found in *Waioli Mission House Grove Farm Homestead: Sixteenth Annual Report, 1989.*

Selective Bibliography

Archival Sources

Dana Hall School Archives, Wellesley
    Class Files

Grove Farm Museum, Kauai
    Grove Farm Plantation Records
    Papers of George N. Wilcox
    Papers of Samuel W. Wilcox
    Papers of Emma Lyman Wilcox
    Papers of Elsie H. Wilcox
    Papers of Mabel I. Wilcox
    Kauai Public Health Oral History Project Transcripts
    Photography Collection
    Grove Farm Museum Files

Hawaii Medical Library, Honolulu
    "In Memorium: Doctors of Hawaii" Files

Hawaii State Archives, Honolulu
    Minutes of the Board of Health

The Johns Hopkins Medical Institutions, Alan Chesney Medical
Archives, Baltimore
    Johns Hopkins Hospital Nurses' Training School Records

Kauai Museum
    Mokihana Club Letters and Reports

Samuel Mahelona Hospital, Kauai
    Minutebook, Board of Trustees

Published Primary Sources

Armbruster, Thomas E., ed. *The Letters and Journals of James William Smith and Melicent Knapp Smith, Medical Missionary Family in Koloa, Kauai, Hawaii.* San Marino High School: San Marino, California, 1999.

Damon, Ethel M., ed. *Letters from the Life of Abner and Lucy Wilcox, 1836-1869.*
Privately published: Honolulu, 1950.

Martin, Margaret G. *Sarah Joiner Lyman: Her Own Story.* Lyman House Memorial Museum: Hilo, Hawaii, 1970

Wedemeyer, Alice C. *The Story of the Mokihana Club of Kauai.*
Privately printed: Kauai, 1987.

Published Secondary Sources

Appleton, V.B. "Report of the Division of Maternal and Infant Hygiene," *Annual Report of the President of the Board of Health of the Territory of Hawaii of the Fiscal Year Ending June 20, 1926,* Honolulu, 1927.

Bushnell, O.A. *The Gifts of Civilization: Germs and Genocide in Hawaii* University of Hawaii Press: Honolulu, 1993

Beyer, Carl Kalani "Manual and Industrial Education for Hawaiians During the 19th Century," *The Hawaiian Journal of History.* 38 2004.

Caldwell, Mark *The Last Crusade: The War on Consumption, 1862-1954.* Atheneum: New York, 1988.

Catton, Margaret M. L. *Social Service in Hawaii.* Pacific Books: Palo Alto, 1959

Damon, Ethel M. *Koamalu: A Story of Pioneers on Kauai and of What They Built in the Garden Island.* Privately Printed: Honolulu, 1931. 2 vols.

Damon, Ethel M. "Mabel Leilani Smyth," *Hawaii Medical Journal and Inter-island Nurses' Bulletin* vol. 16 no. 5 May-June, 1957.

Damon, Ethel M. "Mabel Wilcox, Pioneer in Public Health," *Paradise of the Pacific Annual.* 1952

Daws, Gaven *Holy Man: Father Damien of Molokai.* Harper & Row: New York, 1973.

Duffy, John *The Sanitarians: A History of American Public Health.* University of Illinois Press: Urbana 1990.

Fee, Elizabeth *Disease and Discovery: A History of the Johns Hopkins School of Hygiene and Public Health, 1916-1939.* The Johns Hopkins University Press: Baltimore, 1987.

Griffin, Pat L. *Wilcox Memorial Hospital in the Twentieth Century.* Wilcox Health Foundation: Lihue, 2000.

Grimshaw, Patricia *Paths of Duty: American Missionary Wives in Nineteenth-Century Hawaii.* University of Hawaii Press: Honolulu, 1989.

Hackler, Rhoda E.A. and Yardley, Maili *The History of Kauikeolani Children's Hospital.* Kapiolani Health Care Foundation: Honolulu, 1994.

Harvey, A. McGehee, et. al. *A Model of Its Kind, Volume I: A Centennial History of Medicine at Johns Hopkins.* The Johns Hopkins University Press: Baltimore, 1989.

Hiscock, Ira V. *A Survey of Health and Welfare Activities in Honolulu, Hawaii.* Committee on Administrative Practice, American Public Health Association. Quinnipiack Press: New Haven, 1929.

Hughes, Judith Dean Gething *Women and Children First: The Life and Times of Elsie Wilcox of Kauai.* University of Hawaii Press: Honolulu, 1996.

Johns, Ethel and Pfefferkorn, Blanche *The Johns Hopkins Hospital School of Nursing, 1889-1949.* The Johns Hopkins Press: Baltimore, 1954

Joesting, Edward *Kauai: The Separate Kingdom.* University of Hawaii Press and Kauai Museum Association: Honolulu, 1984.

Kammen, Michael *Mystic Chords of Memory: The Transformation of Tradition in American Culture.* Vintage Books: New York, 1991.

Klaus, Alisa *Every Child a Lion: The Origins of Maternal and Infant Health Policy in the United States and France, 1890-1920.* Cornell University Press: Ithaca, 1993.

Krauss, Bob and Alexander, William P. *Grove Farm Plantation: The Biography of a Hawaiian Sugar Plantation.* Pacific Books: Palo Alto, 1965, 1984.

The Story of Leahi: Fifty Years of Service. Leahi Hospital: Honolulu, 1951.

Legemann, Ellen Condliffe, ed. *Nursing History: New Perspectives, New Possibilities.* Teachers College Press: New York, 1983.

Lewis, Frances R. Hegglund *History of Nursing in Hawaii.* German Kilmer Co.: Node, Wyoming, 1969.

Ludmerer, Kenneth, MD. *Learning to Heal: The Development of American Medical Education.* Basic Books: New York, 1985.

Meckel, Richard A. *Save the Babies: American Public Health Reform and the Prevention of Infant Mortality, 1850-1929.* The Johns Hopkins University Press: Baltimore, 1990.

Nordyke, Eleanor C. *The Peopling of Hawaii.* University of Hawaii Press: Honolulu, 1977.

O'Leary, Margaret R., comp. *Register of the Grove Farm Plantation Records and Papers of George N. Wilcox, Samuel W. Wilcox, Emma L. Wilcox, Elsie H. Wilcox, and Mabel I. Wilcox.* Grove Farm Homestead: Lihue, 1982.

Park, Edwards A., MD., et. al. "A Children's Dispensary Organized on the Basis of Appointments for Patients," *The Modern Hospital.* 13 August, 1919.

Peterson, Barbara B., ed. *Notable Women of Hawaii.* University of Hawaii Press: Honolulu, 1984.

Pickett, Sarah "Nursing Service to the Civilian Population," in Lavina Dock, et. al. *History of American Red Cross Nursing.* Macmillan: New York, 1922.

Reverby, Susan M., *Ordered to Care: The Dilemma of American Nursing, 1850-1945.* Cambridge University Press: Cambridge, 1987.

Riznik, Barnes "From Barracks to Family Homes: A Social History of Labor Housing Reform on Hawaii's Sugar Plantations," *The Hawaiian Journal of History.* 33 1999.

Riznik, Barnes *Waioli Mission House, Hanalei, Kauai.* Grove Farm Homestead and Waioli Mission House: Kauai, 1987.

Rosenberg, Charles *The Care of Strangers: The Rise of America's Hospital System.* Basic Books: New York, 1987.

Russell, Ruth Woodman *Pine Manor: The First Fifty Years, 1911-1961.* Pine Manor Press: Pine Manor, 1969.

Smyth, Mabel L. "Public Health Nursing in Hawaii: A Tribute to Mabel I. Wilcox," *The Pacific Coast Journal of Nursing.* vol. 31, no. 6 June, 1935.

Smyth, Mabel L. "What is a Public Health Nurse?" *First Territorial Conference of Social Work* Honolulu, April 23-29, 1921.

Stannard, David *Before the Horror: The Population of Hawaii on the Eve of Western Contact.* University of Hawaii Press: Honolulu, 1989.

Spenger, Joseph J. *France Faces Depopulation.* Duke University Press: Durham, 1976.

Stevens, Rosemary *In Sickness and In Wealth: American Hospitals in the Twentieth Century.* Basic Books: New York, 1989.

Tucker, Jonathan *Scourge: The Once and Future Threat of Smallpox.* Atlantic Monthly Press: New York, 2001.

van Schaick, John *The Little Corner Never Conquered: The Story of the American Red Cross War Work for Belgium.* Macmillian: New York, 1922.

Wilcox, Elsie *A Record of the Descendants of Abner Wilcox and Lucy Eliza Hart Wilcox, 1836-1950.* Privately Printed: Honolulu, 1950.

Unpublished Secondary Sources

Hulme, Kathryn "They Called Her Wilikoki," typescript, December 18, 1975. Yale University Library.

Kim, Peter, MD. "History of Samuel Mahelona Memorial Hospital," typescript, 1952. Grove Farm museum.

Middleton, Elizabeth H. "History of G.N. Wilcox Memorial Hospital, 1938-1963," typescript, 1963. Grove Farm museum.

Smith, Helen Wong "Nils P. Larsen, M.D., and Plantation Medicine," a paper delivered at Wilcox Hospital, January 10, 1999 in con junction with hospital exhibit "A Tradition of Caring," typescript, 1999. Grove Farm museum.

Riznik, Barnes "Shopping for New England Antiques and Collecting Family Heirlooms in the Restoration of Hawaii's Waioli Mission House," paper delivered at the Dublin Seminar for New England Folklife: New England Collectors and Collections, June 19, 2004. Grove Farm museum.

Index